What People Are Saying about Threshold Bible Study

"This remarkable series provides a method of study and reflection that is bound to produce rich fruit."   Dianne Bergant, C.S.A., Catholic Theological Union, Chicago

"This fine series will provide needed tools that can deepen your understanding of Scripture, but most importantly it can deepen your faith."
     Most Reverend Charles J. Chaput, O.F.M. Cap., Archbishop of Denver

"Threshold Bible Study is a wonderful series that helps modern people read the Bible with insight and joy."   Richard J. Clifford, S.J., Weston Jesuit School of Theology

"The commentary of Stephen Binz does far more than inform; it asks for commitment and assent on the part of the reader/prayer."
     Kathleen O'Connell Chesto, author of *F.I.R.E.* and *Why Are the Dandelions Weeds?*

"This is a wonderful gift for those wishing to make a home for the Word in their hearts."
     Carol J. Dempsey, OP, Associate Professor of Theology, University of Portland, OR

"Written in a sprightly easy-to-understand style, these volumes will engage the mind, heart, and spirit."   Alexander A. Di Lella, O.F.M., The Catholic University of America

"By covering a wide variety of themes and topics, Threshold Bible Study continually breathes new life into ancient texts."
     John R. Donahue, S.J., St. Mary's Seminary and University

"Threshold Bible Study successfully bridges the painful gap between solid biblical scholarship and the rich spiritual nourishment that we expect to find in the words of Scripture."   Demetrius Dumm, O.S.B., Saint Vincent Archabbey

"Threshold Bible Study offers a marvelous new approach for individuals and groups to study themes in our rich biblical and theological tradition."
     John Endres, S.J., Jesuit School of Theology, Berkeley

"Threshold Bible Study enables Catholics to read, with greater understanding, the Bible in the Church."   Francis Cardinal George, O.M.I., Archbishop of Chicago

The LAMB &
The BEASTS

Stephen J. Binz

TWENTY
THIRD 23rd
PUBLICATIONS

The Scripture passages contained herein are from the *New Revised Standard Version of the Bible*, Catholic edition. Copyright ©1989, by the Division of Christian Education of the National Council of Churches in the U.S.A. All rights reserved.

Twenty-Third Publications
A Division of Bayard
One Montauk Avenue, Suite 200
New London, CT 06320
(860) 437-3012 or (800) 321-0411
www.twentythirdpublications.com
ISBN-10: 1-58595-369-5
ISBN 978-1-58595-369-1

Contents

LESSONS 13–18

LESSONS 19–24

LESSONS 25–30

How to Use
Threshold Bible Study

E ach book in the Threshold Bible Study series is designed to lead you
through a new doorway of biblical awareness, to accompany you
across a unique threshold of understanding. The characters, places,
and images that you encounter in each of these topical studies will help you
explore fresh dimensions of your faith and discover richer insights for your
spiritual life.

Threshold Bible Study covers biblical themes in depth in a short amount
of time. Unlike more traditional Bible studies that treat a biblical book or
series of books, Threshold Bible Study aims to address specific topics within
the entire Bible. The goal is not for you to comprehend everything about each
passage, but rather for you to understand what a variety of passages from different books of the Bible reveals about the topic of each study.

Threshold Bible Study offers you an opportunity to explore the entire Bible
from the viewpoint of a variety of different themes. The commentary that
follows each biblical passage launches your reflection about that passage and
helps you begin to see its significance within the context of your contemporary experience. The questions following the commentary challenge you to
understand the passage more fully and apply it to your own life. The prayer
starter helps conclude your study by integrating learning into your relationship with God.

These studies are designed for maximum flexibility. Each study is presented in a workbook format, with sections for reading, reflecting, writing,
discussing, and praying. Space for writing after each question is ideal for
personal study and allows group members to prepare in advance for their
discussion. The thirty lessons in each topic may be used by an individual
over the period of a month, or by a group for six sessions, with lessons to
be studied each week before the next group meeting. These studies are ideal
for Bible study groups, small Christian communities, adult faith formation,

student groups, Sunday school, neighborhood groups, and family reading, as well as for individual learning.

The method of Threshold Bible Study is rooted in the classical tradition of *lectio divina,* an ancient yet contemporary means for reading the Scriptures reflectively and prayerfully. Reading and interpreting the text (*lectio*) is followed by reflective meditation on its message (*meditatio*). This reading and reflecting flows into prayer from the heart (*oratio* and *contemplatio*).

This ancient method assures us that Bible study is a matter of both the mind and the heart. It is not just an intellectual exercise to learn more and be able to discuss the Bible with others. It is, more importantly, a transforming experience. Reflecting on God's word, guided by the Holy Spirit, illumines the mind with wisdom and stirs the heart with zeal.

Following the personal Bible study, Threshold Bible Study offers a method for extending *lectio divina* into a weekly conversation with a small group. This communal experience will allow participants to enhance their appreciation of the message and build up a spiritual community (*collatio*). The end result will be to increase not only individual faith, but also faithful witness in the context of daily life (*operatio*).

Through the spiritual disciplines of Scripture reading, study, reflection, conversation, and prayer, you will experience God's grace more abundantly as your life is rooted more deeply in Christ. The risen Jesus said: "Listen! I am standing at the door, knocking; if you hear my voice and open the door, I will come in to you and eat with you, and you with me" (Rev 3:20). Listen to the Word of God, open the door, and cross the threshold to an unimaginable dwelling with God!

SUGGESTIONS FOR INDIVIDUAL STUDY

• Make your Bible reading a time of prayer. Ask for God's guidance as your read the Scriptures.

• Try to study daily, or as often as possible according to the circumstances of your life.

• Read the Bible passage carefully, trying to understand both its meaning and its personal application as you read. Some persons find it helpful to read the passage aloud.

• Read the passage in another Bible translation. Each version adds to your understanding of the original text.

• Allow the commentary to help you comprehend and apply the scriptural text. The commentary is only a beginning, not the last word on the meaning of the passage.

• After reflecting on each question, write out your responses. The very act of writing will help you clarify your thoughts, bring new insights, and amplify your understanding.

• As you reflect on your answers, think about how you can live God's word in the context of your daily life.

• Conclude each daily lesson by reading the prayer and continuing with your own prayer from the heart.

• Make sure your reflections and prayers are matters of both the mind and the heart. A true encounter with God's word is always a transforming experience.

• Choose a word or a phrase from the lesson to carry with you throughout the day as a reminder of your encounter with God's life-changing word.

• Share your learning experience with at least one other person whom you trust for additional insights and affirmation. The ideal way to share learning is in a small group that meets regularly.

SUGGESTIONS FOR GROUP STUDY

• Meet regularly; weekly is ideal. Try to be on time and make attendance a high priority for the sake of the group. The average group meets for about an hour.

• Open each session with a prepared prayer, a song, or a reflection. Find some appropriate way to bring the group from the workaday world into a sacred time of graced sharing.

• If you have not been together before, name tags are very helpful as a group begins to become acquainted with the other group members.

• Spend the first session getting acquainted with one another, reading the Introduction aloud, and discussing the questions that follow.

• Appoint a group facilitator to provide guidance to the discussion. The role of facilitator may rotate among members each week. The facilitator simply keeps the discussion on track; each person shares responsibility for the group. There is no need for the facilitator to be a trained teacher.

• Try to study the six lessons on your own during the week. When you have done your own reflection and written your own answers, you will be better prepared to discuss the six scriptural lessons with the group. If you have not had an opportunity to study the passages during the week, meet with the group anyway to share support and insights.

• Participate in the discussion as much as you are able, offering your thoughts, insights, feelings, and decisions. You learn by sharing with others the fruits of your study.

• Be careful not to dominate the discussion. It is important that everyone in the group be offered an equal opportunity to share the results of their work. Try to link what you say to the comments of others so that the group remains on the topic.

• When discussing your own personal thoughts or feelings, use "I" language. Be as personal and honest as appropriate and be very cautious about giving advice to others.

• Listen attentively to the other members of the group so as to learn from their insights. The words of the Bible affect each person in a different way, so a group provides a wealth of understanding for each member.

• Don't fear silence. Silence in a group is as important as silence in personal study. It allows individuals time to listen to the voice of God's Spirit and the opportunity to form their thoughts before they speak.

• Solicit several responses for each question. The thoughts of different people will build on the answers of others and will lead to deeper insights for all.

• Don't fear controversy. Differences of opinions are a sign of a healthy and honest group. If you cannot resolve an issue, continue on, agreeing to disagree. There is probably some truth in each viewpoint.

• Discuss the questions that seem most important for the group. There is no need to cover all the questions in the group session.

• Realize that some questions about the Bible cannot be resolved, even by experts. Don't get stuck on some issue for which there are no clear answers.

• Whatever is said in the group is said in confidence and should be regarded as such.

• Pray as a group in whatever way feels comfortable. Pray for the members of your group throughout the week.

Schedule for group study

Session 1: Introduction   Date _____

Session 2: Lessons 1–6   Date _____

Session 3: Lessons 7–12   Date _____

Session 4: Lessons 13–18   Date _____

Session 5: Lessons 19–24   Date _____

Session 6: Lessons 25–30   Date _____

The Lamb at the center of the throne will be their shepherd, and he will guide them to springs of the water of life, and God will wipe away every tear from their eyes. Rev 7:17

The Lamb and the Beasts

In order to understand the book of Revelation, it seems best to imagine the original context in which it was read and heard. We envision ourselves in the city of Ephesus, the capital of the seven cities to which the book was written. In the evening of the first day of the week, "the Lord's day" (Rev 1:10), the Christians assemble in one of the houses of the city to celebrate their weekly Eucharist. They gather to pray, to sing psalms and hymns, to hear the Jewish Scriptures and the new Christian writings, and to share the bread of life and the cup of the new covenant.

As the assembly listens to the new writing of John from the island of Patmos, they are taken on an imaginative journey. Its mystical language evokes wondrous images of Christ: as a luminous being with a long robe and flaming eyes, a triumphant Lamb at the throne of God, and a conquering hero on a white horse whose only weapon is the word of God. The inspired words of John's visions transport the listeners to the throne of the Lamb to worship with all the creatures of heaven who sing songs of triumph and praise. The visions also confront the listener with repulsive images of the violence and injustice that challenge them within the Roman world of the first century. The terrifying images of evil and deception express the insecurity

1

and peril they feel as they face the backbreaking labor, economic anxiety, and intimidating threats of their daily lives.

The purpose of Revelation's visionary journey is to exhort its listeners to faithfulness and to offer them hope. It lays out contrasting visions of the world: the world of the Lamb and the world of the beasts. The central message is this: the Lamb has already conquered the beasts. Our ultimate victory is assured if we choose the Lamb over the beasts and follow in the way of sacrificial, redemptive love. The magnitude of our choice between the Lamb and the beasts is expressed through the inspired imagery of the book. In a sense, we are momentarily given the eyes of God—the eyes to glimpse the heavenly meaning of our worship, to look evil in the face and see its full reality, to gaze upon the cosmic meaning of Christ's sacrifice and victory over sin and death, and to envision the world renewed by the hope for God's kingdom.

Though Revelation is filled with frightening and grotesque images, it is not a book written to instill fear or terror in its listeners. It is a wakeup call, written to increase a sense of urgency for our world. The hope that Revelation offers is not an easy comfort, a passive waiting, or a trouble-free escape. It is a hope that knows the terrors of the world and can still testify to God's absolute love and a promising future. After seeing the deeper realities of creation with God's eyes—where all creation worships around God's throne, where the new Jerusalem is entered through open gates for people of all nations, where all are refreshed by the river of the water of life, and where the tree of life offers healing leaves and nourishing fruit—then we can see all of life more richly and dearly. Revelation gives us the imagination to see the whole world with sacramental vision, to know that God dwells at the heart of creation, and to understand that Christ truly reigns over the world and its future. Once we have glimpsed the world in this way, then the hope that we are given inspires us to commit ourselves to the values of Christ, to work for a more peaceful world, to labor for the healing and reconciliation of people, and to see everyone around us as sacred and beloved of God.

Revelation does not literally predict future events. The warnings given by biblical prophets are always offered for the purpose of conversion; they are offered in order to change God's people. When Jonah went through the city proclaiming God's prophetic word, "Forty days more and Nineveh will be overthrown," God's threatening word was designed to bring the people to repentance. And when the city turned from its evil ways, God did not inflict the calamity his prophet had proclaimed to them (Jon 3:10). God cannot be imprisoned in a predetermined script. Jesus has told us that figuring out the world's future in detail is not God's will for us. He has told us that only the Father knows about the day or the hour (Mark 13:32), and that he will come like a thief (Rev 16:15), without warning or expectation. Revelation is not about what the future holds, but about who holds the future. Thus the best way for a Christian to be ready for the coming of Christ is to stay watchful and keep alert. We need the kind of wakeup calls that Revelation provides, and we need the joyful hope that Revelation inspires.

Reflection and discussion

• How does seeing Revelation as an imaginative journey change my feelings about reading this book?

• What is the difference between end-time speculation and true Christian watchfulness?

Choose Between the Lamb and the Beasts

The focal image of Revelation is the Lamb, a symbol of the risen and glorified Christ. The author draws upon a rich heritage of Israelite and Christian imagery in depicting Christ as God's Lamb. Already in the first book of the Bible, when Isaac asked his father Abraham, "Where is the lamb for the sacrifice," Abraham replied, "God himself will provide the lamb" (Gen 22:8). All of salvation history is really a waiting for the Lamb that God would give to his people. In the story of Exodus, the Israelites sacrificed the Passover lamb on the night of their liberation. The blood of the lamb on their doorposts freed them from the final destructive plague so they could journey to the land promised to them.

In explaining the meaning of Christ's sacrifice, the early Christians looked to the Scriptures of Israel. Isaiah had described the Suffering Servant, a figure who suffered vicariously for God's people, as afflicted and wounded, "like a lamb that is led to the slaughter" (Isa 53:7). John's gospel sums up the ancient sacrificial images of the Old Testament when he calls Jesus "the Lamb of God who takes away the sin of the world" (John 1:29, 36); and Paul uses the same imagery when he calls Jesus the "paschal lamb" who has been sacrificed (1 Cor 5:7). "The Lamb" appears twenty-eight times in the book of Revelation, always as a rich verbal icon of Christ. The Lamb is triumphant, but bearing the marks of his sacrifice, "a Lamb standing as if it had been slaughtered" (5:6). He is given honor and glory by the angels and saints of heaven, and he is followed by the 144,000, whose robes have been washed white in his blood (7:14; 14:4). He conquers the beasts who make war on him (17:14) and his victory is celebrated in the marriage supper of the Lamb (19:7–9).

In opposition to the richly developed image of the Lamb, biblical literature borrows from the mythological literature of the ancient Near East to express the reality of chaos and evil in the symbolic form of beasts. In the Old Testament these primordial beasts represent the powers that threaten God's people. In the book of Job, Leviathan is the repulsive serpent in the sea and Behemoth is an oxlike beast on the earth (Job 40:15—41:34). Throughout the Scriptures of Israel, beasts represent the powers of Israel's enemies, especially the might of Egypt and Babylon. In the visions of Daniel, the great empires of the world and their rulers are depicted as grotesque and ferocious beasts that make war on the people of the earth (Dan 7).

In Revelation, "beast" is used 39 times to refer to the enemies of God's people. The ultimate figure of evil is the fiery red dragon, with seven heads, ten horns, and a destructive tail. The beast that arises from the sea combines all the characteristics of the four beasts in Daniel's vision, thus representing all the political powers that oppress and dehumanize. It receives its authority from the dragon and the whole world worships it. The beast that arises from the land is deceptive, possessing horns like the lamb and speaking like the dragon. It is called the "false prophet" and causes the earth's inhabitants to worship the beast from the sea. The mark of this beast, the number 666, is a distorted imitation of the protective seal placed on the foreheads of God's people. The dragon and its two allied beasts form what some authors have called "a counterfeit trinity." The dragon, the source of all evil, is an anti-God. The first beast, which receives its authority from the dragon, is an anti-Christ. The second beast, which promotes the worship of the anti-Christ beast through trickery, is an anti-Spirit.

Like the Israelites renewing the covenant in the promised land were commanded, "Choose this day whom you will serve" (Josh 24:15), the people of the earth must choose between the Lamb and the beasts. There can be no peaceful coexistence between the worshipers of the satanic dragon and his beastly allies on the one hand and those worshiping God and the Lamb on the other. "Choose this day whom you will serve" is the imperative of the book of Revelation. Counterfeit trinities continue to draw people today to offer their allegiance to movements, desires, and experiences that distort God's will for individuals and for his world. The reign of darkness continues to oppose the kingdom of God. Most importantly, however, for this last book of the Bible, we must know that the Lamb has conquered the beasts. Not only does Revelation proclaim that Christ conquers the empires and global powers that tyrannize and oppress people; he also conquers evil itself and casts it forever into the fiery pit of destruction. The consequence of our choice for the Lamb is nothing less than a share in God's newly created and perfected world.

Reflection and discussion

• Why are institutionalized evil and structural sin depicted as powerful, grotesque beasts in this book?

• Why is Christ depicted as a Lamb throughout this book? How can a gentle Lamb conquer the overwhelming beasts of this world and the underworld?

Retelling the History of Salvation

The book of Revelation can be understood as a retelling of the Bible's principle events of salvation. Choosing the richly symbolic form of apocalyptic literature, the author recaps the two primary events of the Bible: the Exodus of the Old Testament and the Paschal Mystery of the New Testament. Through vivid imagery drawn from both testaments, the author links the contemporary lives of Christians with God's liberation of the Israelites from Egypt and the saving death and resurrection of Jesus Christ.

Revelation unfolds the Exodus story in a new way. The fact that imagery from the Exodus fills the visions of Revelation helps us comprehend the terrible plagues of disasters and death. The seven seals, seven trumpets, and seven bowls echo and intensify the plagues brought against Pharaoh in the Exodus. Hearing the cry of his suffering people, God threatened Egypt with a series of afflictions as part of his overall goal of liberating his people from injustice. The plagues serve for the conversion of the oppressor and the liberation of God's people. The purpose of the threatened tribulations that fill Revelation is to bring about repentance, not to inflict cruelty. The dreadful series of plagues are not a coded script of what is to come in the future, but a frightening warning to bring us to repentance and to wake us up. They exhort us to choose God's vision of life rather than the terrible but inevitable consequences of violent oppression.

The people of God continue to experience a new Exodus throughout history. In the first century, the Christians addressed in John's visions were threatened by the agonies of the beasts, the violent oppression of the Roman empire. Jesus is both the new Moses, leading his people to new life, and the Passover Lamb, the sacrificial victim whose blood was shed for their liberation. The song of Moses, the victory hymn sung by the Israelites after they crossed the sea into freedom, has become in Revelation the song of the Lamb, sung in praise of God's deliverance after the conquest of the beasts (15:3).

Revelation is, above all, a retelling of the story of Jesus' death and resurrection using new images. It is about the heart of the gospel, but told in a new way, through the daring form of apocalyptic literature. It expresses the cosmic significance of the Paschal mystery of Christ's sacrificial death and glorious resurrection, presenting it as a fundamental battle between the forces of good and evil. It is about the struggle of Jesus with the evil powers of this world, their unremitting destruction of him, and his ultimate vindication. The heavenly human being of chapter 1, the slain-yet-standing Lamb of chapter 5, the newborn son of the heavenly woman of chapter 12, and the triumphant rider on the white horse of chapter 19 are all the same person, the crucified and glorified Christ. There is no chronological sequence for these images; they are multiple ways of expressing the meaning of Christ's saving victory in apocalyptic form.

The salvation achieved through the exodus of Israel from slavery and the death and resurrection of Christ is already experienced by people on earth, but the full saving effects of God's victory are not yet fully manifested in the world. In the present time, we are living in the period of tension between the "already" and the "not yet." Revelation lifts the veil that covers our eyes so that we can see the full significance of our salvation. It gives us glimpses, through highly symbolic language, of the full effects of liberation on God's people and the risen life that Christ has won for us.

Reflection and discussion

• In what way is the death and resurrection of Jesus a new exodus for those who follow him?

• How do I experience the tension between the "already" and the "not yet" of God's salvation?

Word, Worship, and Witness

The Word of God. In order to understand the word of God within the words of Revelation, we must realize that its language is symbolic. Symbols allow us to express what cannot be completely expressed in straightforward speech. Our most cherished convictions find their expression in symbolic images and actions. Think of the cross, the flag, your ring. Symbols affect us at a level deeper than intellectual understanding. They do not simply communicate information; they take hold of us and elicit powerful emotions and convictions.

Revelation is not a code book; it is a symphony of images. It is important that we read it with our imaginations engaged. Attempts to express images and symbols in logical, factual language rob them of their rich meaning and power of persuasion. Revelation should be approached more like a work of art than a mathematical problem. Interpreting symbolic language is less a rational act than an act of the imagination. We can gain hints at the meaning of the book's many symbolic numbers, colors, places, and creatures by understanding the meaning of similar symbolism in other parts of the Bible and other first-century Jewish and Christian literature. While there are plenty of authors today who want to tell us what Revelation "really" means, we can never express the full meaning of its imagery in conceptual language, nor should we ever try.

Though Revelation was probably not the last book of the Bible written, it is appropriate that the book was chosen by the church to be the last book of the Bible. As the Bible begins with God's creation in the book of Genesis, it ends with God's new creation in Revelation. The work demonstrates that Jesus Christ is the summit of salvation history. As the book proclaims, he is "the Alpha and the Omega, the first and the last, the beginning and the end" (22:13). Christ is the originator of the universe—through him all things were made; and he is the goal of the universe—through him all things are fulfilled. More than any other book of the New Testament, this work is filled with words, images, and symbols that have their roots in the Old Testament, but it expresses them in a whole new way. In Christ, what God has been doing throughout history comes to its climactic completion.

From Word to Worship. Revelation expresses the dynamic interaction between word and worship, a relationship in which the worship enacts the word and the word explains the worship. Worship is a large part of the content and message of Revelation as well as its context. It is the central act both in heaven and on earth. John describes his visionary experience: "I was in the spirit on the Lord's day" (1:10), probably meaning that he was worshiping the Lord on Sunday. As he worships he experiences his visions, and what he envisions, at all the key moments throughout his book, is essentially worship. The liturgical images and acts that pervade the book are provided by both the emerging tradition of Christian eucharistic worship in the first century and the ancient tradition of Israelite temple liturgy.

The immediate context in which the visionary message of John was heard by the Christian assembly was the Sunday Eucharist. In the sacred space of worship, heaven and earth connect. In sacred time, the past, present, and future merge. The eucharistic assembly is, at the same time, a present experience of Christian worship, a re-enactment of the last supper of Jesus with his disciples, and an anticipation of the messianic banquet at the end of time. In the context of worship, we can assemble in the sacred space of the Eucharist, gather with John on the island of Patmos, and stand before the throne to worship God in heaven.

Worship transcends time, as it brings the past and the future into the present moment. "The Lord's day," in the context of worship, is simultaneously the present day on which the Christians assemble, the first Easter on which Christ rose from the dead, and that future "day of the Lord," the coming day of justice of which the prophets spoke. The reading of Revelation in the context of worship enables the listener to experience the one "who is and who was and who is to come" (1:8). Jesus came to them in the past in his saving death and resurrection; he comes to them in the inspired words of John and in the Eucharist they share; and Jesus will come to them for the complete manifestation of his reign. The liturgical acclamation of the Christian assembly, "Come, Lord Jesus" (22:20), is a prayer for the present moment as well as for the ultimate future, all within the timeless moment of worship.

From Worship to Witness. Revelation also demonstrates the necessary relationship between worship and witness. The reading of Revelation within the context of worship bound the hearers together into a community of shared vision. Their own worship of God and the Lamb, in contrast to the earthly worship of the beasts, expressed what was supreme for them and what held power to influence and direct their lives. Worship provided the vision of the Lamb's victory, a conviction that empowered his followers to struggle on, to resist the lure of evil, to live in hope, to witness that the Lamb has conquered the beasts.

As Christians we bring every part of our daily lives to our worship. The experience of worship cannot be simply an addition to daily life; rather it must be an intensification of it. Witness in the world is the ongoing task of the church as it awaits the coming of the Lord. The witness and testimony of Christian disciples is an essential part of God's plan for the world's salvation. The conquest of the dragon and the coming of God's kingdom are accomplished "by the blood of the Lamb and by the word of their testimony" (Rev 12:11). It is the sacrificial action of Christ on the cross, along with the witness to Christ through the living testimony of believers, that brings about God's desired salvation for the world. Everything that we say and do that is truly Christ-like and faithful to him is a witness to the world of God's truth. The most effective witness is the quality of our Christian lives, working toward that new Jerusalem, held out as a vision of what God's world can be and will be. Assured of victory we work toward that day when "the kingdom of the world has become the kingdom of our Lord and of his Messiah" (11:15).

Reflection and discussion

• In what way does worshiping God help me see the truth of my life and believe that truth more securely?

• How does my worship empower me to be a witness for Christ in my daily life?

Reading the Book of Revelation

Let us place ourselves in the lamp-lit darkness as Christians gather to worship. As we listen to the words of God's prophet John, we are taken on a visionary journey with him. In another level of existence, we meet the risen Christ, participate in the heavenly liturgy before God's throne, witness the attack of the ancient dragon, and are shown the true meaning of Christ's conquest through his saving death. The experience transforms our self-identity. We are engaged as participants in the battle of Christ against the beasts. We are changed from victims of oppressive circumstances to victors with Christ over the ultimate forces of evil. As we prepare to experience the Eucharist, we hear the voice of Jesus himself saying, "See, I am coming soon" (22:12, 20). Gathered around the Lord's table, we experience the coming of Jesus, a coming already made known from the past, a coming anticipated in the future, and a coming that is known in the present—charging our lives with cosmic significance and forming us into faithful witnesses and victors.

Reading great literature demands nearly as much imagination from the reader as creating it demands of the author. As you begin to study this work, forget what you have heard in the past about the book of Revelation. Realize that the work does not give predictions about future events; much less does it offer a timetable for the end of the world. Free your imagination from the chains of literalism. Imagine yourself listening among the assembled Christians, hearing this work for the first time. Read it aloud, so that you can truly hear the words and the visions may come to life in your imagination. You will feel the difference.

Prayer

Lamb of God, who frees us from sin by your own blood, have mercy on us. You are worthy to receive power and wealth and wisdom and might and honor and glory and blessing. During this study, teach me to follow you and to be your faithful witness. Protect me from the powers of evil and show me how to make my life a testimony to your love and truth. Guide, encourage, and enlighten me as I read and contemplate your inspired word.

SUGGESTIONS FOR FACILITATORS, GROUP SESSION 1

1. If the group is meeting for the first time, or if there are newcomers joining the group, it is helpful to provide nametags.

2. Distribute the books to the members of the group.

3. You may want to ask the participants to introduce themselves and tell the group a bit about themselves.

4. Ask one or more of these introductory questions:
   - What drew you to join this group?
   - What is your biggest fear in beginning this Bible study?
   - How is beginning this study like a "threshold" for you?

5. You may want to pray this prayer as a group:

Come upon us, Holy Spirit, to enlighten and guide us as we begin this study of the apocalyptic images of Revelation. You gave your servant John the prophetic message and told him to write down his visions. As we experience this visionary journey, work deeply within us, to change us and give us hope. Motivate us to read the Scriptures and give us a deeper love for God's word each day. As we experience the word, lead us to worship and witness. Bless us during this session and throughout the coming week with the fire of your love.

6. Read the Introduction aloud, pausing at each question for discussion. Group members may wish to write the insights of the group as each question is discussed. Encourage several members of the group to respond to each question.

7. Don't feel compelled to finish the complete Introduction during the session. It is better to allow sufficient time to talk about the questions raised than to rush to the end. Group members may read any remaining sections on their own after the group meeting.

8. Instruct group members to read the first six lessons on their own during the six days before the next group meeting. They should write out their own answers to the questions as preparation for next week's group discussion.

9. Fill in the date for each group meeting under "Schedule for Group Study."

10. Conclude by praying aloud together the prayer at the end of the Introduction.

Blessed is the one who reads aloud the words of the prophecy, and blessed are those who hear and who keep what is written in it; for the time is near.

Rev 1:3

The Revelation of Jesus Christ

REVELATION 1:1–8 ¹ *The revelation of Jesus Christ, which God gave him to show his servants what must soon take place; he made it known by sending his angel to his servant John, ²who testified to the word of God and to the testimony of Jesus Christ, even to all that he saw.*

³Blessed is the one who reads aloud the words of the prophecy, and blessed are those who hear and who keep what is written in it; for the time is near.

⁴John to the seven churches that are in Asia:

Grace to you and peace from him who is and who was and who is to come, and from the seven spirits who are before his throne, ⁵and from Jesus Christ, the faithful witness, the firstborn of the dead, and the ruler of the kings of the earth.

To him who loves us and freed us from our sins by his blood, ⁶and made us to be a kingdom, priests serving his God and Father, to him be glory and domin-ion forever and ever. Amen.

⁷Look! He is coming with the clouds;
　　every eye will see him,

even those who pierced him;
and on his account all the tribes of the earth will wail.
So it is to be. Amen.
      [8]*"I am the Alpha and the Omega," says the Lord God, who is and who was*
and who is to come, the Almighty.

The opening word of the original Greek text is the word *apokalypsis,* which provides the title of the book. The word is commonly translated as "revelation," but its literal meaning is "uncovering." The work will uncover what is hidden to the Christian community, the deeper truths of what God is doing in the world. Apocalyptic literature was flourishing in the surrounding culture at the time, and Jewish writers had been producing apocalyptic works for over two centuries by the time John wrote. The features of this type of literature include visions, angelic messengers, numerical symbolism, otherworldly journeys, cosmic battles between God and his enemies, and portraits of judgment and blessings. Because his readers were so familiar with this type of writing, John's work would not have sounded nearly as strange to his original audience as it does to us. In fact, there is evidence that announcing revelations was a regular part of Christian worship (1 Cor 14:6, 26).

In addition to calling his work an apocalypse, John also designates it as "prophecy" (verse 3). The meaning of prophecy is not, as is so commonly assumed in modern culture, a prediction of the future. Prophecy, in the ancient world, was the communication of a message from God. Though it could involve warnings and expectations about the future, it was essentially a message for the present situation. John says that his work concerns "what must soon take place" (verse 1). He affirms the urgency of his message with the comment that "the time is near" (verse 3). Clearly the prophecy is not a revelation relegated to the distant future; it is a pressing communication for the present moment.

Though God is the ultimate source of Revelation, John does not get his revelation directly from God. Rather it proceeds through a chain of transmission: God gave it to Jesus, who in turn gave it, through his angel, to John, who then communicates it to God's servants, the Christian community (verse 1). John sends his message in the form of a letter to seven churches in the Roman province of Asia (today's western Turkey, verse 4). He wants his message to be read aloud in the Christian assembly, and he wants the listeners to truly hear what is proclaimed and take it to heart (verse 3).

Grace and peace are from God, "him who is and who was and who is to come," and from God's Spirit, and from Jesus Christ (verses 4–5). This trinitarian salutation describes God as ever-present, an expansion of God's self-designation in Exodus as "I Am" (Exod 3:14). "The seven spirits" before God's throne express the manifold activities of the one Holy Spirit. The number seven expresses divine fullness and here refers to the seven designations of God's Spirit in the Greek version of Isaiah 11:2—the spirit of wisdom, understanding, counsel, strength, knowledge, piety, and fear of the Lord. Jesus Christ is "the faithful witness" *par excellence* through his sacrificial death, "the firstborn of the dead" in his resurrection, and "the ruler of the kings of the earth" as he reigns in glory.

The acclamations of praise (verses 5–7) are addressed to the risen Christ and celebrate the continuing love he manifested in his redeeming death—he freed us by his blood. His death made possible a new relationship with God. We are now "a kingdom, priests serving our God," a dignity promised to God's people at Mount Sinai (Exod 19:5). The one "coming with the clouds" who will be seen by all, "even those who pierced him," combines images from the prophetic texts of the Old Testament (Dan 7:13; Zech 12:10). The coming one will be universally recognized, even by those who put him to death. The liturgical language of the acclamations and the repeated "amen" response suggests a community gathered for worship.

Reflection and discussion

• What indicates to me that Revelation is not a prediction of some distant future?

• What does it mean to me that God is the one "who is and who was and who is to come"? What does it mean to me that this God offers me grace and peace?

• What three things does Jesus do for us (verses 5–6)?

• Which of these titles and images for God and Jesus Christ mean the most to me? Which could I incorporate into my prayer?

Prayer

Alpha and Omega, you are the one who is and who was and who is to come. Give me your Spirit of wisdom and understanding as I ponder your word. Reveal yourself to me and give me your grace and your peace.

Do not be afraid; I am the first and the last, and the living one. I was dead, and see, I am alive forever and ever; and I have the keys of Death and of Hades. Now write what you have seen, what is, and what is to take place after this. Rev 1:17–19

A Vision on the Lord's Day

REVELATION 1:9–20 *⁹I, John, your brother who share with you in Jesus the persecution and the kingdom and the patient endurance, was on the island called Patmos because of the word of God and the testimony of Jesus. ¹⁰I was in the spirit on the Lord's day, and I heard behind me a loud voice like a trumpet ¹¹saying, "Write in a book what you see and send it to the seven churches, to Ephesus, to Smyrna, to Pergamum, to Thyatira, to Sardis, to Philadelphia, and to Laodicea."*

¹²Then I turned to see whose voice it was that spoke to me, and on turning I saw seven golden lampstands, ¹³and in the midst of the lampstands I saw one like the Son of Man, clothed with a long robe and with a golden sash across his chest. ¹⁴His head and his hair were white as white wool, white as snow; his eyes were like a flame of fire, ¹⁵his feet were like burnished bronze, refined as in a furnace, and his voice was like the sound of many waters. ¹⁶In his right hand he held seven stars, and from his mouth came a sharp, two-edged sword, and his face was like the sun shining with full force.

¹⁷When I saw him, I fell at his feet as though dead. But he placed his right

*hand on me, saying, "Do not be afraid; I am the first and the last, [18] and the liv-
ing one. I was dead, and see, I am alive forever and ever; and I have the keys of
Death and of Hades. [19] Now write what you have seen, what is, and what is to
take place after this. [20] As for the mystery of the seven stars that you saw in my
right hand, and the seven golden lampstands: the seven stars are the angels of the
seven churches, and the seven lampstands are the seven churches."*

John now turns to the circumstances of his revelation and his call to write
it down and send it to the seven churches. He tells us that he was on the
island of Patmos, a rocky island off the coast of the Roman province of
Asia—a place where the Romans banished their political prisoners. John was
probably exiled here because of his witness to Christ. In addressing his soli-
darity with his readers, John refers to the Christian life as "persecution," "the
kingdom," and "patient endurance" (verse 9), capturing the paradoxical
nature of our life in Christ. We share in God's kingdom while at the same
time experiencing distress and tribulation. This contradictory condition
requires consistent resistance and steadfast perseverance, a challenge that
John seeks to evoke in his readers throughout the book.

On a Sunday, "the Lord's day," John was "in the spirit" and heard a trum-
pet-like voice (verse 10) telling him to write down what he sees and to send
it to the seven churches (verse 11). When he turned to see whose voice he
had heard, he saw the first of many visions we will encounter in Revelation
(verses 12–16). The vision is a composite of Old Testament images (especially from Daniel 7 and 10), evoking a sense of the majesty of the risen
Christ. The elements of John's description—his clothing, his hair, his eyes,
feet, and voice—are biblical symbols expressing the priesthood, kingship,
eternity, and divinity of Christ. We are not meant to visualize every detail of
the vision, nor should we try to translate every element of the vision into a
specific meaning. Rather we should allow the elements of the vision to evoke
multiple meanings, associations, and emotions so that we experience more
deeply realities that we cannot fully understand.

The risen Christ is envisioned in the midst of seven golden lampstands and
holding seven stars in his right hand. John helps us with our interpretation of
the vision by offering us the clue that the seven stars are the angels of the
seven churches, and the seven lampstands are the seven churches (verse 20).
The images express the heavenly and the earthly nature of the church.

Followers of Jesus stands on earth giving light to the world with Christ in their midst, but they already share in Christ's victory and eternity's glory.

The clear message offered by the glorified Christ is "Do not be afraid" (verse 17). Though he was crucified, he now lives forever (verse 18). He has reversed the poles of life and death, so that his followers, even if they die, will live. For that reason, those suffering trials and tribulations need not fear that death will separate them from his saving love. The gloriously risen Christ is our hope and our source of endurance.

Reflection and discussion

• What thoughts and feelings does the vision of verses 13 to 16 evoke in me?

• In what way does the church have both an earthly and a heavenly reality? In what way do I participate in this dual nature of Christ's church?

Prayer

Glorious Lord, you are the living one who holds the keys of death. When I worship on the Lord's day, help me to contemplate the grandeur of your risen presence with me. May that vision of your glorious life empower me to witness your presence throughout the week.

Be faithful until death, and I will give you the crown of life. Let anyone who has an ear listen to what the Spirit is saying to the churches. Rev 2:10–11

A Message for the Seven Churches

REVELATION 2:1–11 *¹"To the angel of the church in Ephesus write: These are the words of him who holds the seven stars in his right hand, who walks among the seven golden lampstands:*

²"I know your works, your toil and your patient endurance. I know that you cannot tolerate evildoers; you have tested those who claim to be apostles but are not, and have found them to be false. ³I also know that you are enduring patiently and bearing up for the sake of my name, and that you have not grown weary. ⁴But I have this against you, that you have abandoned the love you had at first. ⁵Remember then from what you have fallen; repent, and do the works you did at first. If not, I will come to you and remove your lampstand from its place, unless you repent. ⁶Yet this is to your credit: you hate the works of the Nicolaitans, which I also hate. ⁷Let anyone who has an ear listen to what the Spirit is saying to the churches. To everyone who conquers, I will give permission to eat from the tree of life that is in the paradise of God.

⁸"And to the angel of the church in Smyrna write: These are the words of the first and the last, who was dead and came to life:

⁹"I know your affliction and your poverty, even though you are rich. I know the slander on the part of those who say that they are Jews and are not, but are a synagogue of Satan.[10]*Do not fear what you are about to suffer. Beware, the devil is about to throw some of you into prison so that you may be tested, and for ten days you will have affliction. Be faithful until death, and I will give you the crown of life.* [11]*Let anyone who has an ear listen to what the Spirit is saying to the churches. Whoever conquers will not be harmed by the second death.*

John's inaugural vision of the risen Christ contains seven letters addressed to the angels of each of the seven churches listed at the beginning of the vision (1:11). The angels are the guardians or heavenly counterparts of the earthly churches. The seven churches are separated by about a day's journey, forming a circuit starting at Ephesus, the closest city to Patmos. Though each letter was addressed to a separate church, every church was expected to read the other six letters. Each church was a historical community of the first century, but the symbolic number seven evokes the fullness of Christ's church. Thus, the message delivered to them is also the word of God to us.

Each letter is remarkably alike in structure. Each begins with a characteristic of Christ from John's first vision (verses 2, 8; also 2:12, 18; 3:1, 7, 14). This connects each letter directly back to John's visionary experience and relates a unique aspect of Christ to particular aspects of the church in each city. The conclusion of each letter offers a promise for those who "conquer" (verses 7, 10–11; see also 2:17, 26–28; 3:5, 12, 21). These seven assurances anticipate images from visions toward the end of the work. In this way, both the beginning and the end of the letters reflect aspects of the visionary journey taken by the hearers in each church as they listen to the words of Revelation.

The opening words of Christ in every letter, "I know…" (verses 3, 9), indicate that Christ knows the special circumstances of each community. He offers words of commendation for faithfulness and criticism for unfaithfulness. The particulars vary for each of the churches. The apocalyptic images that will fill the remainder of John's work will reflect aspects of the conflict, failures, betrayals, and victories in the ongoing life of every one of the seven churches.

Ephesus was the most prominent of the seven cities, most known for its great temple to the goddess Artemis and its temple to the Roman emperors. Paul had ministered there for several years, and it is probable that the gospel and letters of John were written from this same community. Christ praises the church for their patient endurance and their rejection of false apostles and teachers (verses 2–3, 6). He then chastens them: "You have abandoned the love you had at first" (verse 4). The original fervor of love for Christ and for fellow believers had grown cold. Christ urges them to "repent" and to "do the works you did at first" (verse 5).

Smyrna lay thirty-five miles north of Ephesus up the coast. The city was a center for the ritual worship of the emperor and was most famous for its wealth, fine buildings, and devotion to science and medicine. The church receives no criticism, only praise. They were experiencing poverty and affliction, but Christ reminds them of their great wealth in heavenly riches (verse 9). It seems that they were also experiencing "slander" from some of the Jews in the city. The Jewish Christians considered themselves the true heirs of the heritage of Israel, resulting in hostility between the Christian and Jewish population of the city. Christ's exhortations to them are two: "do not fear," despite the coming sufferings, afflictions, and imprisonment, and "be faithful until death" (verse 10). Those who remain faithful are promised "the crown of life" and preservation from harm by "the second death," the final judgment.

Reflection and discussion

• What combination of praise and criticism would my church receive from Christ if he were to address a prophetic letter to us?

• Have I lost the fervent love I once had for Christ and those who share my faith (verse 4)? What steps can I take to return to a more passionate love?

• How can the church in Smyrna be both poor and rich (verse 9)? In what ways am I rich?

• How faithful would I be in the midst of trials and persecution for my beliefs? Have I ever received a test of my faithfulness?

Prayer

Crucified and risen Christ, you bring life and victory from the furnace of trial and suffering. Give me the strength to endure the testing in my life, and the courage to remain always faithful to you.

All the churches will know that I am the one who searches minds and hearts, and I will give to each of you as your works deserve. Rev 2:23

Love, Faith, Service, and Patient Endurance

REVELATION 2:12–29 ¹²*"And to the angel of the church in Pergamum write: These are the words of him who has the sharp two-edged sword:*

¹³ *"I know where you are living, where Satan's throne is. Yet you are holding fast to my name, and you did not deny your faith in me even in the days of Antipas my witness, my faithful one, who was killed among you, where Satan lives.* ¹⁴*But I have a few things against you: you have some there who hold to the teaching of Balaam, who taught Balak to put a stumbling block before the people of Israel, so that they would eat food sacrificed to idols and practice fornication.* ¹⁵*So you also have some who hold to the teaching of the Nicolaitans.* ¹⁶*Repent then. If not, I will come to you soon and make war against them with the sword of my mouth.* ¹⁷*Let anyone who has an ear listen to what the Spirit is saying to the churches. To everyone who conquers I will give some of the hidden manna, and I will give a white stone, and on the white stone is written a new name that no one knows except the one who receives it.*

¹⁸*"And to the angel of the church in Thyatira write: These are the words of the Son of God, who has eyes like a flame of fire, and whose feet are like burnished bronze:*

[19]*"I know your works—your love, faith, service, and patient endurance. I know that your last works are greater than the first.* [20]*But I have this against you: you tolerate that woman Jezebel, who calls herself a prophet and is teaching and beguiling my servants to practice fornication and to eat food sacrificed to idols.* [21]*I gave her time to repent, but she refuses to repent of her fornication.* [22]*Beware, I am throwing her on a bed, and those who commit adultery with her I am throwing into great distress, unless they repent of her doings;* [23]*and I will strike her children dead. And all the churches will know that I am the one who searches minds and hearts, and I will give to each of you as your works deserve.* [24]*But to the rest of you in Thyatira, who do not hold this teaching, who have not learned what some call 'the deep things of Satan,' to you I say, I do not lay on you any other burden;* [25]*only hold fast to what you have until I come.* [26]*To everyone who conquers and continues to do my works to the end,*

I will give authority over the nations;
[27]*to rule them with an iron rod,*
as when clay pots are shattered—
[28]*even as I also received authority from my Father. To the one who conquers I will also give the morning star.* [29]*Let anyone who has an ear listen to what the Spirit is saying to the churches.*

Pergamum lay fifty miles north of Smyrna and about fifteen miles inland from the sea, with its citadel situated on a hill towering over the surrounding valley. The city was renowned in the ancient world for its library and book production and contained numerous temples to the gods. It was especially known as a center for the worship of Asclepius, the god of healing, giving the city widespread acclaim as an important medical center. The symbol of Asclepius was the serpent, which is today depicted on the caduceus, the insignia of physicians. Within John's Hebrew mindset, however, the serpent was a symbol of evil and the powers of Satan (12:9). The city was also the first in Asia to build a temple to the emperor and was preeminent in the cult of the emperor. On both counts Pergamum could be called "Satan's throne" and the place "where Satan lives" (verse 13).

Christ both praises and chides the church in Pergamum. They are commended for holding fast during times of hostility to Christians and for not denying their faith. At least one from among them, named Antipas, was killed for his fidelity, earning him the designation "my witness" (or martyr). The church is criticized for its accommodation to those who would allow an easy coexistence with the practices of the pagan world, like allowing Christians to participate in worship of the emperor and to eat meat sacrificed to idols. These practices are characterized as "the teaching of Balaam" (verse 14). Balaam was a Moabite prophet from the time of the exodus. He incited the Israelites to have sexual relations with the women of Moab and to worship their gods. He is chosen here as the Old Testament prototype for the kind of false teachings the Christians have to resist in order to be faithful to Christ.

Thyatira lay forty miles southeast of Pergamum. The city was noteworthy for its large number of trade guilds, many of them associated with the textile industry. Paul's first convert in Philippi was Lydia, a dealer in purple cloth from Thyatira (Acts 16:14). Each of these guilds was associated with the temples of the gods, and anyone who did not participate in these guilds was unable to make a living. As in most of these cities, the underlying dispute seems to be over the extent to which Christians could participate in Roman civic and economic life, since it involved at least nominal worship of the Roman gods.

Christ praises the church for their "love, faith, service, and patient endurance" (verse 19). But he reprimands the church for tolerating the teachings of "that woman Jezebel" (verse 20), a derisive name for a false prophet who is leading the church "to practice fornication and to eat food sacrificed to idols." The name Jezebel is an allusion to the wicked wife of the Old Testament king Ahab. She had attempted to exterminate God's prophets and lead Israel into the worship of other gods. "Fornication" and "adultery" (verses 14, 20, 22) are used in a metaphorical sense, both here and by Israel's ancient prophets, to refer to the infidelity demonstrated in the worship of foreign gods and moral compromise with pagan culture. The harsh threats of punishment are given in order to encourage Jezebel and her followers to "repent" while there is still time (verses 21–22). The later visions of the great harlot (Rev 17–18) will demonstrate the great evil at the root of the practices of Jezebel. The menacing language challenges us to look at our contemporary society through the eyes of Christ, to clear away our deceptions, and to change our hearts. How far have we compromised the truth of God's Lamb to the standards and practices of the contemporary world?

As in all seven letter, those who conquer are promised a share in God's new creation. The "hidden manna" (verse 17), the eucharistic bread of life, will sustain the victors in place of the "food sacrificed to idols" (verses 14, 20). The "white stone" upon which is written "a new name" will admit its holders into the heavenly banquet of the new Jerusalem. Those remaining faithful will also share in Christ's authority over the nations and his victory over death, symbolized by "the morning star" (verses 26–28; 22:16).

Reflection and discussion

• Why does Revelation use the Old Testament figure of Balaam and Jezebel to describe the practices of first-century churches?

• In what ways were the pressures of being a Christian in the first century similar to the pressures of today?

Prayer

> *Son of God, you know my successes and accomplishments in doing good in your name; you also know my failures and sins. Give me courage in my struggles to do your will, and help me to discern the positive and negative influences of the culture in which I live.*

Remember then what you received and heard; obey it, and repent. If you do not wake up, I will come like a thief, and you will not know at what hour I will come to you. Rev 3:3

Let No One Seize Your Crown

REVELATION 3:1–13 ¹ *"And to the angel of the church in Sardis write: These are the words of him who has the seven spirits of God and the seven stars:*

"I know your works; you have a name for being alive, but you are dead. ² *Wake up, and strengthen what remains and is at the point of death, for I have not found your works perfect in the sight of my God.* ³ *Remember then what you received and heard; obey it, and repent. If you do not wake up, I will come like a thief, and you will not know at what hour I will come to you.* ⁴ *Yet you have still a few people in Sardis who have not soiled their clothes; they will walk with me, dressed in white, for they are worthy.* ⁵ *If you conquer, you will be clothed like them in white robes, and I will not blot your name out of the book of life; I will confess your name before my Father and before his angels.* ⁶ *Let anyone who has an ear listen to what the Spirit is saying to the churches.*

⁷ *"And to the angel of the church in Philadelphia write:*
These are the words of the holy one, the true one,
  who has the key of David,
  who opens and no one will shut,
    who shuts and no one opens:

⁸*"I know your works. Look, I have set before you an open door, which no one is able to shut. I know that you have but little power, and yet you have kept my word and have not denied my name.* ⁹*I will make those of the synagogue of Satan who say that they are Jews and are not, but are lying—I will make them come and bow down before your feet, and they will learn that I have loved you.* ¹⁰*Because you have kept my word of patient endurance, I will keep you from the hour of trial that is coming on the whole world to test the inhabitants of the earth.* ¹¹*I am coming soon; hold fast to what you have, so that no one may seize your crown.* ¹²*If you conquer, I will make you a pillar in the temple of my God; you will never go out of it. I will write on you the name of my God, and the name of the city of my God, the new Jerusalem that comes down from my God out of heaven, and my own new name.* ¹³*Let anyone who has an ear listen to what the Spirit is saying to the churches.*

The circuit of the seven churches continues: Sardis lay thirty miles southeast of Thyatira. Rising high above the valley, it was thought to be virtually impregnable. However, the city suffered two surprising defeats in its ancient history because it was caught off guard by its enemies. The city also suffered a devastating earthquake in AD 17, but was quickly rebuilt and remained an important commercial center. The warning that Christ will come to them like a thief if they do not wake up (verse 3) must have been a particularly sobering reminder of their past history. The harsh words of Christ to the church in Sardis indicate that their outward appearance was different from the truth of their lives. In sharp contrast to Christ "who was dead and came to life" (1:18; 2:8), they have a reputation for "being alive," but they are really "dead" (verse 1). Despite their good reputation, their works seem to be half-hearted and half-done. Christ calls them to change using five sharp admonitions: wake up, strengthen what remains, remember how you accepted the gospel, obey it, and repent (verses 2–3). Since they cannot know the time of Christ's coming, they must shake off their apathy and remain vigilant.

Philadelphia lay thirty miles southeast of Sardis, at the intersection of several trade routes. Christ's words to them contain only praise and promises. Despite their small number and limited resources, they have remained faithful to the "word" and "name" of Christ (verse 8). Their "open door" refers to their opportunities for spreading the gospel in Asia Minor, in the sense that their example presents a motive for others to enter the church.

Their missionary zeal, however, was met with opposition from some of the Jewish population of the city (verse 9). Yet in time, the Jews will honor those who follow Christ because they will realize that he has loved them. As a reward for their faithfulness, Christ will protect them during the time of the coming trial and testing (verse 10).

Those who conquer by remaining faithful will receive a share in the fullness of life to come. They will be clothed in white robes and have their names in the book of life (verse 5). They will be a pillar in the temple of the new Jerusalem, and they will be inscribed with the name of God and with Christ's new name (verse 12). The images anticipate the later visions of the new Jerusalem in which God will dwell with his people.

Reflection and discussion

• When do I notice myself becoming complacent, half-hearted, and apathetic? What does Christ's call to wake up, to be watchful, and to remain vigilant mean practically for my life?

• What "open door" has Christ placed before me? What should I do with that open door?

Prayer

Risen Lord, you call your people to receive the good news of your life and to spread it to others. Make me watchful and alert so that I may use every daily opportunity to express my love for you. Do not subject me to the trial but deliver me from the evil one.

Listen! I am standing at the door, knocking; if you hear my voice and open the door, I will come in to you and eat with you, and you with me. Rev 3:20

Waiting at the Threshold

REVELATION 3:14–22 ¹⁴*"And to the angel of the church in Laodicea write: The words of the Amen, the faithful and true witness, the origin of God's creation:*

¹⁵*"I know your works; you are neither cold nor hot. I wish that you were either cold or hot.* ¹⁶*So, because you are lukewarm, and neither cold nor hot, I am about to spit you out of my mouth.* ¹⁷*For you say, 'I am rich, I have prospered, and I need nothing.' You do not realize that you are wretched, pitiable, poor, blind, and naked.* ¹⁸*Therefore I counsel you to buy from me gold refined by fire so that you may be rich; and white robes to clothe you and to keep the shame of your nakedness from being seen; and salve to anoint your eyes so that you may see.* ¹⁹*I reprove and discipline those whom I love. Be earnest, therefore, and repent.* ²⁰*Listen! I am standing at the door, knocking; if you hear my voice and open the door, I will come in to you and eat with you, and you with me.* ²¹*To the one who conquers I will give a place with me on my throne, just as I myself conquered and sat down with my Father on his throne.* ²²*Let anyone who has an ear listen to what the Spirit is saying to the churches."*

Laodicea completes the circle of cities to which the seven messages were delivered. It lay about forty miles southeast of Philadelphia and ninety miles east of Ephesus. The city was famous as a banking center, as a woolen manufacturing center, and for its medical school. The church receives the harshest judgment of all, without a word of commendation. The church is accused of being "lukewarm," "neither hot nor cold" (verses 15–16). Hot water has its value for bathing and healing; cold water for quenching and refreshment. Tepid water, however, has no value; it is merely spit out of the mouth. The residents of Laodicea would have clearly understood this image of water temperature. Colossae, a few miles to the east, was supplied with cold water from the Lycus River, but by the time it reached Laodicea by aquaduct, the water was tepid. Hierapolis, a city to the north, was famous for its natural hot springs, but by the time the waters reached Laodicea, they were naturally lukewarm. The faith of the church there, likewise, had become indifferent, lukewarm, and compromising. Such faith means nothing; it accomplishes nothing; it inspires no one.

Furthermore, the church arrogantly thinks of itself as wealthy, prosperous, and self-sufficient. But Christ chastens it for being "poor, blind, and naked" (verse 17). Each element of the triple counsel of Christ (verse 18) stands as an ironic counterpart to something about which the city of Laodicea boasted. First, in contrast to the city's status as a banking center, the church is urged to buy from Jesus "gold refined by fire" if they want to be truly rich. Second, though the city was famous for producing textiles made from black wool, the church is urged to obtain white robes from Jesus to cover their nakedness. Third, in a region well known for its therapeutic powder for the healing of eyes, the church is urged to anoint their eyes with the salve of Jesus if they want to truly see.

The purpose of all Christ's harsh warnings is to get the people of his church to repent and change their ways: "I reprove and discipline those whom I love" (verse 19). Out of love, Jesus makes his richest promise to the only church about whom he can find nothing good to say. Though he threatens to spit them out of his mouth, he has not yet done so. Christ waits and delays; he exhorts his people and offers them time to repent. Jesus is "standing at the door knocking" (verse 20). We can imagine a door that has no handle on the outside; it must be opened from within. He is waiting for his people to open. The people of Laodicea, like us, still have the opportunity to hear his knocking and invite him inside. Jesus does not force himself on anyone; he awaits the invitation to enter. When we open the door, Christ promises to come into our lives and share his sacred meal, the banquet of life, with us.

The letters close with the final promise to those who conquer: "I will give a place with me on my throne" (verse 21; 20:4). Just as Christ conquered and sat with the Father on his throne, the Christian who is faithful will rule with Christ. This image, like all the promises offered to each of the faithful in the churches, will be further expanded as John takes the seven churches on the visionary journey to come.

All seven letters of prophecy end with the cry, "Let anyone who has an ear listen to what the Spirit is saying to the churches" (verse 22). That cry is addresses to all who would read John's work, including all of us today. The seven churches provide examples of the kinds of things that can go wrong in any church. Christ continues to praise and admonish his church through his Spirit. The visions to come are a prophetic word to all God's people as we await the coming of the Lord in glory.

Reflection and discussion

• Why is lukewarm water such an effective symbol for the faith of the Laodiceans?

• What is the water temperature of my faith?

• Has affluence made me blind or made me think I am self-sufficient? What is Christ's invitation to me?

• What is Jesus waiting for at the door of my life? How can I open the door and let him in today?

• Which words to the seven churches speak most directly to my situation? In what way do they challenge me?

Prayer

Lord, you are seated on the throne of God and you promise me a place with you if I am faithful. You see all aspects of my life, where I have accomplished your will and where I need to change. Challenge me, refine me, and give me a deeper zeal to follow you. I open the door and invite you to dwell in my life forever.

SUGGESTIONS FOR FACILITATORS, GROUP SESSION 2

1. If there are newcomers who were not present for the first group session, introduce them now.

2. You may want to pray this prayer as a group:

Lord Jesus Christ, you offer us a glorious vision of yourself through the revelation of your servant, John. You walk amid the seven lampstands and hold the seven stars in your hand. Your eyes are like a flame of fire, you are clothed in a white robe, and a sharp sword comes from your mouth. You penetrate into the heart of the seven churches and into the soul of each one here. Through the visionary journey of John you want to change us and you urge us to repent. Open our hearts to the word of God, allow it to pierce our inner being, and give us the courage to change our lives.

3. Ask one or more of the following questions:
   • What was your biggest challenge in Bible study over this past week?
   • What did you learn about yourself this week?

4. Discuss lessons 1 through 6 together. Assuming that group members have read the Scripture and commentary during the week, there is no need to read it aloud. As you review each lesson, you might want to briefly summarize the Scripture passages of each lesson and ask the group what stands out most clearly from the commentary.

5. Choose one or more of the questions for reflection and discussion from each lesson to talk over as a group. You may want to ask group members which question was most challenging or helpful to them as you review each lesson.

6. Keep the discussion moving, but don't rush the discussion in order to complete more questions. Allow time for the questions that provoke the most discussion.

7. Instruct group members to complete lessons 7 through 12 on their own during the six days before the next group meeting. They should write out their own answers to the questions as preparation for next week's group discussion.

8. Conclude by praying aloud together the prayer at the end of lesson 6, or any other prayer you choose.

Coming from the throne are flashes of lightning, and rumblings and peals of thunder, and in front of the throne burn seven flaming torches, which are the seven spirits of God. Rev 4:5

Worship At the Throne of God

REVELATION 4:1–11 ¹*After this I looked, and there in heaven a door stood open! And the first voice, which I had heard speaking to me like a trumpet, said, "Come up here, and I will show you what must take place after this." ²At once I was in the spirit, and there in heaven stood a throne, with one seated on the throne! ³And the one seated there looks like jasper and carnelian, and around the throne is a rainbow that looks like an emerald. ⁴Around the throne are twenty-four thrones, and seated on the thrones are twenty-four elders, dressed in white robes, with golden crowns on their heads. ⁵Coming from the throne are flashes of lightning, and rumblings and peals of thunder, and in front of the throne burn seven flaming torches, which are the seven spirits of God; ⁶and in front of the throne there is something like a sea of glass, like crystal.*

Around the throne, and on each side of the throne, are four living creatures, full of eyes in front and behind: ⁷the first living creature like a lion, the second living creature like an ox, the third living creature with a face like a human face, and the fourth living creature like a flying eagle. ⁸And the four living creatures, each of them with six wings, are full of eyes all around and inside. Day and night without ceasing they sing,

"Holy, holy, holy,
the Lord God the Almighty,
who was and is and is to come."
[9] *And whenever the living creatures give glory and honor and thanks to the one*
who is seated on the throne, who lives forever and ever, [10] *the twenty-four elders*
fall before the one who is seated on the throne and worship the one who lives for-
ever and ever; they cast their crowns before the throne, singing,
[11] *"You are worthy, our Lord and God,*
to receive glory and honor and power,
for you created all things,
and by your will they existed and were created."

J ohn's visionary ascent to the throne of God in heaven shows us the heavenly counterpart to the church on earth. His passage through the open door into heaven reveals a marvelous world in which all creation worships God. The heavenly liturgy is the fullness of reality behind the Eucharist and Christian witness of the seven churches. This two-leveled world, the church on earth and the worship of God in heaven, exists simultaneously, and the events on earth can only be fully understood in conjunction with their heavenly counterpart.

Human language is clearly incapable of expressing the infinite realities of God. So John's language is full of symbols and metaphors to express the grandeur and glory of God. As he enters the heavenly world, the visionary first sees the throne and the one seated upon it. The imagery alludes to the Old Testament descriptions of the inmost sanctuary of the temple. There God sat invisibly enthroned on the ark of the covenant between two angelic creatures. The prophet Micaiah claimed a similar experience: "I saw the Lord sitting on his throne, with all the hosts of heaven standing beside him to the right and to the left of him" (1 Kgs 22:19). John carefully avoids any descriptive details of God; even word pictures of God are forbidden in the Old Testament tradition of Israel. God is far beyond any attempts to capture the divine presence in images. Precious gems—shining, sparkling, and radiant—express the glory of God (verse 3). They refract a rainbow of prismatic colors, the sign of God's covenant with creation (Gen 9:13–16).

The "twenty-four elders," seated on thrones, wearing white robes, and wearing crowns of gold (verse 4), are the twelve patriarchs of Israel and the twelve apostles. Together they represent the old and new covenants—all the people of God. The lightening and thunder recall the manifestation of God on Mount Sinai (Exod 20:18) and express God's powerful majesty (verse 5). The seven flaming torches express the fullness of God's Spirit. The "four living creatures" (verse 6) represent all the living beings of creation. Resembling a lion, an ox, a human being, and a flying eagle, they symbolize what is noblest, strongest, wisest, and swiftest in creation. In the second century these four became associated with the writers of the four gospels.

The vision is reminiscent of many passages in the Old Testament, especially the opening chapter of Ezekiel and the call of Isaiah in chapter 6. Everything revolves around the one seated on the throne. Day and night, age after age, the worship of God never ceases. God is not one power among many; God is almighty (verse 8). God is the creator of all that is (verse 11). There is nothing in the heavens or on the earth or under the earth that can hold sway against God. The one seated on the throne is great beyond all imagining, and even a glimpse of God's majesty and power should bring us to our knees to sing in jubilant adoration with all the creatures of heaven.

Reflection and discussion

• In what ways does this vision help me to contemplate God's presence and worship God's majesty?

• Why does John not attempt to describe the one seated upon the throne? Why does he give us a vision of God seen through a kaleidoscope rather than through a telescope?

• In what way do the four living creatures demonstrate that all creation praises its Creator?

• What is the resemblance between this heavenly scene and the church's earthly liturgy?

• The adoration of God is the highest form of prayer and the deepest fulfillment of his creation. How much of my prayer consists of adoration of God for who he is and what he has done?

Prayer

Holy, holy, holy, Lord God the Almighty, who was and is and is to come.
You are the creator of all and you sustain all things in being. I give you
honor, glory, and thanks, and I long to dwell in your presence forever.

When he had taken the scroll, the four living creatures and the twenty-four elders fell before the Lamb, each holding a harp and golden bowls full of incense, which are the prayers of the saints. Rev 5:8

Worthy Is the Lamb

REVELATION 5:1–14 *¹Then I saw in the right hand of the one seated on the throne a scroll written on the inside and on the back, sealed with seven seals; ²and I saw a mighty angel proclaiming with a loud voice, "Who is worthy to open the scroll and break its seals?" ³And no one in heaven or on earth or under the earth was able to open the scroll or to look into it. ⁴And I began to weep bitterly because no one was found worthy to open the scroll or to look into it. ⁵Then one of the elders said to me, "Do not weep. See, the Lion of the tribe of Judah, the Root of David, has conquered, so that he can open the scroll and its seven seals."*

⁶Then I saw between the throne and the four living creatures and among the elders a Lamb standing as if it had been slaughtered, having seven horns and seven eyes, which are the seven spirits of God sent out into all the earth. ⁷He went and took the scroll from the right hand of the one who was seated on the throne. ⁸When he had taken the scroll, the four living creatures and the twenty-four elders fell before the Lamb, each holding a harp and golden bowls full of incense, which are the prayers of the saints. ⁹They sing a new song:

"You are worthy to take the scroll
and to open its seals,
for you were slaughtered and by your blood you ransomed for God

saints from every tribe and language and people and nation;
   [10] *you have made them to be a kingdom and priests serving our God,*
      and they will reign on earth."
   [11] *Then I looked, and I heard the voice of many angels surrounding the throne and the living creatures and the elders; they numbered myriads of myriads and thousands of thousands,* [12] *singing with full voice,*
   "Worthy is the Lamb that was slaughtered
   to receive power and wealth and wisdom and might
   and honor and glory and blessing!"
[13] *Then I heard every creature in heaven and on earth and under the earth and in the sea, and all that is in them, singing,*
   "To the one seated on the throne and to the Lamb
   be blessing and honor and glory and might
   forever and ever!"
[14] *And the four living creatures said, "Amen!" And the elders fell down and worshiped.*

Continuing the heavenly vision of God's throne, our attention is turned to the scroll in God's right hand, sealed with seven seals (verse 1). The scroll contains God's plan to redeem the world, to bring all creation to its completion. A search throughout all creation finds no one worthy to open the scroll—that is, to carry out God's plan for the world's salvation (verses 2–3). Then one of the elders declares that "the Lion of the tribe of Judah" could open the scroll because he has "conquered" (verse 5). The Lion of Judah and the Root of David are references from the Hebrew Scriptures pointing to the coming Messiah.

When John looked to see the Lion, the most powerful of all beasts, instead he sees a Lamb with the marks of slaughter upon it (verse 6). He looked to see power and ferocious force, by which the enemies of faith would be conquered, but he sees sacrificial love and gentleness as the way to victory. Rather than the lion who tears his prey, Jesus is the torn Lamb. There is violence for sure, but it is endured not inflicted. Jesus has conquered through his death and resurrection. Like the gospel image in which the risen Christ bears the marks of his suffering, the Lamb is "standing as if it had been slaughtered." Its seven horns are an ironic indication of the Lamb's power; its seven eyes show that Jesus fully possesses the Spirit of God (verse 6; 1:4).

The scroll that the Lamb received from the throne of God does not only refer to events of the future. God's plan to redeem the world is already being accomplished. It began at the cross and continues until the coming of Christ in glory. The Lamb has already conquered (verse 5), not will conquer some-day; he has already ransomed for God saints from every nation (verse 9). What we hear proclaimed in the unfolding of the scroll is a symbolic descrip-tion of what is already in the process of taking place, not what will happen only at the end of time.

The scene of God's throne (Rev 4) and this scene of the glorious Lamb are parallel visions. First God is revealed in glory and worshiped, then Christ is revealed and worshiped. The four living creatures and twenty-four elders bow down before the Lamb (verse 8). The prayers of the saints both in heav-en and on earth are symbolized by the incense (Ps 141:2), indicating that the church on earth worships with the assembly of heaven in adoration of God and the Lamb. The "new song" proclaims the new saving action that God has done in and through the slain Lamb and why the Lamb is "worthy to take the scroll and to open its seals." The first round is sung by the living creatures and elders (verses 9–10). Like the blood of the Passover lamb which protected the Israelites from the plague of death, the blood of the Lamb of God ransomed people of every language and nation and made them a kingdom and priests. Every disciple of Jesus shares in the universal redemption and the royal priesthood of Christ. The second round is joined by a countless throng of angels singing with full voice (verses 11–12). They express a seven-fold praise of the Lamb: power, wealth, wisdom, might, honor, glory, and blessing. The climactic round is sung by every creature—the whole universe (verse 13). Their praise is directed jointly to God and to the Lamb. The worshiping community on earth is joined by the whole cos-mos in divine liturgy.

Reflection and discussion

• In what way does this vision express the cross and resurrection of Jesus from the viewpoint of heaven?

• Why is Jesus depicted as a Lamb rather than a Lion? What are the implications for the way he conquers?

• Why is the Lamb alone worthy to take the scroll and open its seals?

• What are the implications of the cosmic liturgy for my Sunday worship? What does it matter that the angels and saints of heaven praise God with me?

Prayer

Eternal Lamb of God, you are indeed worthy to receive honor, glory, and might. With your blood you ransomed me from slavery to sin and death. May I praise you always with all the creatures of heaven and earth.

I saw under the altar the souls of those who had been slaughtered for the word of God and for the testimony they had given. Rev 6:9–10

Opening the Seven Seals

REVELATION 6:1–17 ¹*Then I saw the Lamb open one of the seven seals, and I heard one of the four living creatures call out, as with a voice of thunder, "Come!"* ²*I looked, and there was a white horse! Its rider had a bow; a crown was given to him, and he came out conquering and to conquer.*

³*When he opened the second seal, I heard the second living creature call out, "Come!"* ⁴*And out came another horse, bright red; its rider was permitted to take peace from the earth, so that people would slaughter one another; and he was given a great sword.*

⁵*When he opened the third seal, I heard the third living creature call out, "Come!" I looked, and there was a black horse! Its rider held a pair of scales in his hand,* ⁶*and I heard what seemed to be a voice in the midst of the four living creatures saying, "A quart of wheat for a day's pay, and three quarts of barley for a day's pay, but do not damage the olive oil and the wine!"*

⁷*When he opened the fourth seal, I heard the voice of the fourth living creature call out, "Come!"* ⁸*I looked and there was a pale green horse! Its rider's name was Death, and Hades followed with him; they were given authority over a fourth of the earth, to kill with sword, famine, and pestilence, and by the wild animals of the earth.*

⁹*When he opened the fifth seal, I saw under the altar the souls of those who had been slaughtered for the word of God and for the testimony they had given;* ¹⁰*they cried out with a loud voice, "Sovereign Lord, holy and true, how long will it be before you judge and avenge our blood on the inhabitants of the earth?"* ¹¹*They were each given a white robe and told to rest a little longer, until the number would be complete both of their fellow servants and of their brothers and sisters, who were soon to be killed as they themselves had been killed.*

¹²*When he opened the sixth seal, I looked, and there came a great earthquake; the sun became black as sackcloth, the full moon became like blood,* ¹³*and the stars of the sky fell to the earth as the fig tree drops its winter fruit when shaken by a gale.* ¹⁴*The sky vanished like a scroll rolling itself up, and every mountain and island was removed from its place.* ¹⁵*Then the kings of the earth and the magnates and the generals and the rich and the powerful, and everyone, slave and free, hid in the caves and among the rocks of the mountains,* ¹⁶*calling to the mountains and rocks, "Fall on us and hide us from the face of the one seated on the throne and from the wrath of the Lamb;* ¹⁷*for the great day of their wrath has come, and who is able to stand?"*

The vision centers on the sealed scroll, which we should imagine as a lengthy sheet of papyrus rolled into a tube and bound with seven tied ribbons, each of which is sealed with a wax impression. As the Lamb opens each seal, John witnesses corresponding events happen on the earth. The opening of the first six seals is described here in sequence.

The first four seals follow the same pattern: the Lamb opens the seal; one of the four living creatures around the throne calls out, "Come"; John sees a colored horse; and its rider is described. The four form a consistent series of events associated with violent conquest, a sequence that has often been acted out in history. The opening of the first seal reveals a white horse and a rider carrying a bow, the characteristic weapon of earthly conquerors. He received a crown for his violent and dubious victory (verse 2). The opening of the second seal reveals a bright red horse and a rider with a huge sword. The rider took away the false and fragile peace that existed between nations under the Roman empire and provoked international strife and bloodshed (verses 3–4). The opening of the third seal reveals a black horse and a rider carrying a pair of scales needed to weigh food during a time of famine. The payment of a day's wages for a supply of grain indicates a desperate food crisis (verses 5–6). The opening of the fourth seal reveals a pale green horse and a rider named Death, along with his companion Hades. Their killing takes many forms, including sword, famine, pestilence, and wild animals (verses 7–8). The colors of the four horses vividly express the devastation brought on by human violence and injustice: conquest, bloodshed, famine, and death. They represent the social reality experienced in the Roman world of the first century, yet clearly these four horsemen continue to ride across the earth today. Without social justice, then hatred, greed, and violence inevitably create social chaos upon the earth.

The fifth seal reveals the souls of those who shed their blood in witness to the word of God (verse 9). These Christian martyrs are seen "under the altar." The image alludes to the altar of sacrifice in the Jerusalem temple at the base of which the lifeblood of the sacrificed animals was poured out. This image indicates that the death of these Christian witnesses is interpreted as a sacrifice to God. The martyrs cry out to God, "How long?" (verse 10), seeking an end to the madness represented by the four horsemen and seeking judgment on those who had shed their blood. They are given "white robes" of victory and told to rest until God's appointed time (verse 11). There will be more persecution and martyrdom to come before the Lamb's victory is complete.

The sixth seal unfolds an abundance of apocalyptic signs and presents a scene of terrible tribulation (verses 12–14). The vision is a collage of Old Testament imagery: the great earthquake (Hag 2:6), the blackened sun and the moon like blood (Joel 2:31), and the sky rolled up like a scroll (Isa 34:4). It is as if all the images of Israel's prophets for the terrible day of the Lord are shown at once. The foundations of God's creation are coming undone and the powerful ones of the earth attempt in vain to hide from God because they know their sin (verses 15–16; Gen 3:8). "The wrath of the Lamb" is an image filled with irony, the mistaken interpretation of those who reject God's invitation to repent. From the point of view of the oppressor, the plagues seem wrathful; from the point of view of the oppressed, the plagues seem liberating.

The images of suffering and dread, like the images of wonder and glory, are all part of John's visionary journey. The descriptions are intended to provoke repentance and radical change in the hearts of those who hear them. The opening of the six seals describes the terror of an unrepentant world and the inevitable judgment of social sin and injustice. But in the midst of the world's suffering, the merciful, redemptive Lamb is renewing the earth.

Reflection and discussion

• In what ways do the four horsemen continue to ride across the earth today?

• Have I ever experienced God as wrathful? How was this view a result of my limited vision and understanding?

• Do the terrors of our world conflict with my understanding of the mercy and forgiveness of God's Lamb?

Prayer

Sovereign Lord, holy and true, how long will you allow the injustices and suffering of our world to continue? I pray that your will be done on earth as it is in heaven, and that you make me an instrument of your peace.

These are they who have come out of the great ordeal; they have washed their robes and made them white in the blood of the Lamb. For this reason they are before the throne of God, and worship him day and night within his temple. Rev 7:14–15

Washed in the Blood of the Lamb

REVELATION 7:1–17 ¹*After this I saw four angels standing at the four corners of the earth, holding back the four winds of the earth so that no wind could blow on earth or sea or against any tree. ²I saw another angel ascending from the rising of the sun, having the seal of the living God, and he called with a loud voice to the four angels who had been given power to damage earth and sea, ³saying, "Do not damage the earth or the sea or the trees, until we have marked the servants of our God with a seal on their foreheads."*

⁴*And I heard the number of those who were sealed, one hundred forty-four thousand, sealed out of every tribe of the people of Israel:*

⁵*From the tribe of Judah twelve thousand sealed,*
from the tribe of Reuben twelve thousand,
from the tribe of Gad twelve thousand,
⁶*from the tribe of Asher twelve thousand,*
from the tribe of Naphtali twelve thousand,

from the tribe of Manasseh twelve thousand,
⁷*from the tribe of Simeon twelve thousand,*
from the tribe of Levi twelve thousand,
from the tribe of Issachar twelve thousand,
⁸*from the tribe of Zebulun twelve thousand,*
from the tribe of Joseph twelve thousand,
from the tribe of Benjamin twelve thousand sealed.

⁹*After this I looked, and there was a great multitude that no one could count, from every nation, from all tribes and peoples and languages, standing before the throne and before the Lamb, robed in white, with palm branches in their hands.* ¹⁰*They cried out in a loud voice, saying,*

"Salvation belongs to our God who is seated on the throne, and to the Lamb!"
¹¹*And all the angels stood around the throne and around the elders and the four living creatures, and they fell on their faces before the throne and worshiped God,* ¹²*singing,*

"Amen! Blessing and glory and wisdom
and thanksgiving and honor
and power and might
be to our God forever and ever! Amen."
¹³*Then one of the elders addressed me, saying, "Who are these, robed in white, and where have they come from?"* ¹⁴*I said to him, "Sir, you are the one that knows." Then he said to me, "These are they who have come out of the great ordeal; they have washed their robes and made them white in the blood of the Lamb.*

¹⁵*For this reason they are before the throne of God,*
and worship him day and night within his temple,
and the one who is seated on the throne will shelter them.
¹⁶*They will hunger no more, and thirst no more;*
the sun will not strike them,
nor any scorching heat;
¹⁷*for the Lamb at the center of the throne will be their shepherd,*
and he will guide them to springs of the water of life,
and God will wipe away every tear from their eyes."

Before the opening of the seventh seal, John is given two visions—the first (verses 1–8) an earthly vision, and the second (verses 9–17) a heavenly one. Both visions offer assurance and comfort to God's people in the midst of the sufferings and terrors on the earth.

Four angels at the four corners of the earth are holding back the winds of destruction from all four directions (verse 1). Another angel from the East brings "the seal of the living God" to be placed on the foreheads of God's servants (verses 2–3). As the scroll becomes unsealed, God's elect are sealed. In the ancient world, a royal seal was used to mark the property of a king. The seal indicates that the persecuted church belongs to God and is under his protection. The image evokes the protective mark of the Passover in which the blood of the lamb designated the Hebrew families so that the angel of death would pass over them (Exod 12). The image also reminds the hearer of the vision of Ezekiel in which God commanded an angel to mark the foreheads of those citizens of Jerusalem who rejected idolatry. Those marked would be protected from the judgment of the city (Ezek 9:4–6). The idea of sealing was a widely used metaphor in early Christianity, most often connected with the Holy Spirit and baptism (2 Cor 1:22; Eph 1:13). The seal does not symbolize immunity from suffering and death; rather it assures the faithful that they have nothing to fear because of their divine possession and protection.

Those who receive God's seal are twelve thousand from each of the twelve tribes of Israel (verses 4–8). Early Christianity stressed its continuity with Israel as the elect "people of God." The letter of James, written to Christians scattered throughout the Roman empire, addresses them as "the twelve tribes in the dispersion" (Jas 1:1). Paul referred to the church as the restored "Israel of God" (Gal 6:16). The 144,000 is not a literal number, but represents the whole people of God. In ancient Israel, a census of the twelve tribes was designed to count those available for military service (Num 1). In Revelation, this army of the Lamb is a parody of the violent power of the Roman army. They fight with the weapons of love and conquer by giving witness to the Lamb.

The second vision imagines those "who have come out of the great ordeal" (verse 14), those who endured and remained faithful to the end. They are described as "a great multitude that no one could count" from every nation, race, and language (verse 9). Clad in white, with palms of victory in their hands, they stand before the throne and the Lamb, acknowledging God and the Lamb as the source of their salvation (verse 10). The white robes of the great multitude have been washed and made white "in the blood of the Lamb" (verse 14). This incongruous image expresses the reality that Christ's death is the source of their victory. The closing images are a poetic expression of salvation (verses 15–17). God and the Lamb meet all the physical and emotional needs of each faithful witness as they worship. God shelters them in his presence and wipes away the tears of earthly grief. The Lamb becomes the shepherd, guiding his flock to the waters of life.

Both of these visions describe the faithful people of God, one from the viewpoint of earth and the other from heaven. The militant church on earth, the Israel of God, is the future worshiping assembly of heaven. The 144,000 on earth is the great heavenly multitude that no one could count. Both visions reveal to the seven churches of Asia and to all of us the hidden meaning of our struggles and the hope for which we yearn.

Reflection and discussion

• How does the seal on the foreheads of the elect express God's possession and protection?

• In what way has God placed his seal upon me? How do I experience God's protection?

• How can the robes of God's elect become white when washed in the blood of the Lamb?

• Whom have you seen wearing a white robe? What do the white robes seem to represent?

• What indicates that 144,000 is a symbolic number rather than a statistic?

Prayer

Victorious Lord, I have nothing to fear in the midst of my life's sufferings and uncertainties. I am marked with the seal of your Holy Spirit for my ultimate protection. You will shepherd me into your presence and wipe away every tear from my face.

The angel took the censer and filled it with fire from the altar and threw it on the earth; and there were peals of thunder, rumblings, flashes of lightning, and an earthquake. Rev 8:5

Seven Angels With Seven Trumpets

REVELATION 8:1–13 *¹When the Lamb opened the seventh seal, there was silence in heaven for about half an hour. ²And I saw the seven angels who stand before God, and seven trumpets were given to them.*

³Another angel with a golden censer came and stood at the altar; he was given a great quantity of incense to offer with the prayers of all the saints on the golden altar that is before the throne. ⁴And the smoke of the incense, with the prayers of the saints, rose before God from the hand of the angel. ⁵Then the angel took the censer and filled it with fire from the altar and threw it on the earth; and there were peals of thunder, rumblings, flashes of lightning, and an earthquake.

⁶Now the seven angels who had the seven trumpets made ready to blow them.

⁷The first angel blew his trumpet, and there came hail and fire, mixed with blood, and they were hurled to the earth; and a third of the earth was burned up, and a third of the trees were burned up, and all green grass was burned up.

⁸The second angel blew his trumpet, and something like a great mountain, burning with fire, was thrown into the sea. ⁹A third of the sea became blood, a third of the living creatures in the sea died, and a third of the ships were destroyed.

¹⁰*The third angel blew his trumpet, and a great star fell from heaven, blazing like a torch, and it fell on a third of the rivers and on the springs of water.* ¹¹*The name of the star is Wormwood. A third of the waters became wormwood, and many died from the water, because it was made bitter.*

¹²*The fourth angel blew his trumpet, and a third of the sun was struck, and a third of the moon, and a third of the stars, so that a third of their light was darkened; a third of the day was kept from shining, and likewise the night.*

¹³*Then I looked, and I heard an eagle crying with a loud voice as it flew in midheaven, "Woe, woe, woe to the inhabitants of the earth, at the blasts of the other trumpets that the three angels are about to blow!"*

The opening of the seventh seal brings total silence for half an hour (verse 1). It is a brief silence of anticipation, like the stillness before the storm. Into this eerie hush comes an angel with a golden censer (verse 3), and the smoke of incense accompanies the prayers of God's people that rise up to God's throne. All in heaven and the church on earth pray in response to what they have seen and heard.

The seven angels who stand before God (verse 2) form a particular group, called the "angels of the presence" in Jewish tradition. One of these seven is identified in the book of Tobit: "I am Raphael, one of the seven angels who stand ready and enter before the glory of the Lord" (Tob 12:15). The other six, according to the apocryphal book of Enoch, are Uriel, Rauel, Michael, Sariel, Gabriel, and Remiel. These seven are given seven trumpets, announcing the next series of warnings.

The welcome and contemplative silence is shattered as an angel casts the censer full of hot coals to the earth (verse 5) and the trumpets sound in succession. The sequence of images throughout Revelation is not linear but spiral; each series of events offers new images for the same reality and the same message. This new series of seven is more severe than the preceding series, involving a third of all creation—not a total devastation. The trumpet warnings not only use many of the same images as the ten plagues of the exodus, they also serve the same purpose. The calamities that threaten Rome and its emperor in John's day are like those that threatened Egypt and its pharaoh at the time of the Israelite exodus (Exod 7–10).

The first trumpet brings hail and fire (verse 7), recalling the seventh plague against the Egyptians, heavy hail upon the land with flashes of fire (Exod 9:22–25). The second trumpet evokes the image of the great mountain burning with fire (verse 8), recalling Mount Sinai and possibly the volcanic eruptions of the first century. The sea that turns to blood (verse 9) is an adaptation of the first plague of the exodus, the river that turns to blood (Exod 7:17–21). Egypt had depended on the Nile River for irrigation and commerce, but Rome depended on the Mediterranean Sea. Whereas the exodus plague focused on the fish in the river, the second trumpet highlighted the creatures of the sea and the commercial ships. The third trumpet brings a burning star that falls to earth and causes the rivers and springs to become bitter (verse 10–11). This recalls the bitter water discovered along the journey of the exodus (Exod 15:23) and an oracle given by Jeremiah against the people's infidelity (Jer 9:15). The fourth trumpet brings darkness over the earth (verse 12), recalling the ninth Egyptian plague (Exod 10:21–23).

The catastrophes that threatened the oppressive society of John's day are like those that struck Egypt for refusing to allow the Israelites to go free. The trumpets are warnings designed to bring a change of heart, as were the ten plagues of Egypt. It is less important to understand all the particulars of the plagues than to feel their power and dreadfulness. These images are not realistic, of course, but are part of the cumulative effect of John's visionary journey.

Reflection and discussion

• What is the effect of the silence at the opening of the seventh seal? In what way is silence a form of prayer and worship?

• In what ways does Revelation compare the emperor of Rome to the pharaoh of Egypt?

• What is the purpose of these shocking images in the overall plan of Revelation?

• Reflect on the terrible evils of our world: terrorism, starvation, torture, genocide, war. Do I burn with anger, as does God, at these evils and cry out for justice?

Prayer

> *God of all nations, in my comfort and security, let me not forget my brothers and sisters who suffer daily because of the injustice and neglect of others. Help me respond to your warnings and cooperate with your saving plan for the world.*

They have as king over them the angel of the bottomless pit; his name in Hebrew is Abaddon, and in Greek he is called Apollyon. Rev 9:11

A Demonic Plague of Locusts

REVELATION 9:1–21 *¹And the fifth angel blew his trumpet, and I saw a star that had fallen from heaven to earth, and he was given the key to the shaft of the bottomless pit; ²he opened the shaft of the bottomless pit, and from the shaft rose smoke like the smoke of a great furnace, and the sun and the air were darkened with the smoke from the shaft. ³Then from the smoke came locusts on the earth, and they were given authority like the authority of scorpions of the earth. ⁴They were told not to damage the grass of the earth or any green growth or any tree, but only those people who do not have the seal of God on their foreheads. ⁵They were allowed to torture them for five months, but not to kill them, and their torture was like the torture of a scorpion when it stings someone. ⁶And in those days people will seek death but will not find it; they will long to die, but death will flee from them.*

⁷In appearance the locusts were like horses equipped for battle. On their heads were what looked like crowns of gold; their faces were like human faces, ⁸their hair like women's hair, and their teeth like lions' teeth; ⁹they had scales like iron breastplates, and the noise of their wings was like the noise of many chariots with horses rushing into battle. ¹⁰They have tails like scorpions, with stingers, and in their tails is their power to harm people for five months. ¹¹They have as king over them the angel of the bottomless pit; his name in Hebrew is Abaddon, and in Greek he is called Apollyon.

¹²The first woe has passed. There are still two woes to come.

¹³Then the sixth angel blew his trumpet, and I heard a voice from the four horns of the golden altar before God, ¹⁴saying to the sixth angel who had the trumpet, "Release the four angels who are bound at the great river Euphrates." ¹⁵So the four angels were released, who had been held ready for the hour, the day, the month, and the year, to kill a third of humankind. ¹⁶The number of the troops of cavalry was two hundred million; I heard their number. ¹⁷And this was how I saw the horses in my vision: the riders wore breastplates the color of fire and of sapphire and of sulfur; the heads of the horses were like lions' heads, and fire and smoke and sulfur came out of their mouths. ¹⁸By these three plagues a third of humankind was killed, by the fire and smoke and sulfur coming out of their mouths. ¹⁹For the power of the horses is in their mouths and in their tails; their tails are like serpents, having heads; and with them they inflict harm.

²⁰The rest of humankind, who were not killed by these plagues, did not repent of the works of their hands or give up worshiping demons and idols of gold and silver and bronze and stone and wood, which cannot see or hear or walk. ²¹And they did not repent of their murders or their sorceries or their fornication or their thefts.

Until now, John's visions have revealed a two-tiered world, with images focusing on both earth and heaven. But his declaration that no one "in heaven or on earth or under the earth" (5:3) was able to open the scroll hints that reality should be imagined as a three-storied universe. Not only does John see a door that leads him into heaven (4:1), but he is also shown a shaft that leads to the abyss, "the bottomless pit" (verses 1–2). When the fallen angel unlocks the shaft, smoke is released and fearsome creatures arise. This angel of the underworld rules over the abyss like a king, and his name is Destruction and Destroyer (verse 11). Earth is perched precariously between the kingdom of heaven and the kingdom of the bottomless pit. And so like any small nation between two large adversaries, we can expect the earth to be the place of battle.

The fifth and sixth in the series of trumpets, like the fifth and sixth seals, are more detailed and more terrifying than the first four. As the fifth trumpet sounds, the bottomless pit is opened, and a plague of demonic locusts is unleashed (verse 3). Locusts were one of the most feared scourges of ancient times. A locust swarm could strip a land of its crops within days, leaving a famine behind. They appear as the eighth plague sent on Egypt at the exodus (Exod 10:12–15). The prophet Joel depicted a locust swarm as a symbol of God's judgment on Israel (Joel 1–2). The locusts here are described as a terrifying army: like horses ready for battle, with human faces, teeth like lions, chests of iron, wings that sound like chariots, tails that sting like scorpions (verses 7–10). Their destruction is unleashed against those to bring suffering and oppression upon God's people. Those who have God's seal on their foreheads, along with the trees and vegetative growth of the earth, remain unharmed (verse 4). In the early church, part of the effects of baptism was understood to be a seal of protection against the attacks of Satan, giving us a share in Christ's authority over the assaults of evil.

The sixth trumpet sounds and two hundred million cavalry troops are released. The fire, smoke, and sulfur, represented by the red, blue, and yellow breastplates of the troops, destroy a third of the human race (verses 16–18). They are released by four angels held in bonds until this moment (verse 15). God does not create evil, but allows at this moment the powers of evil to rage unchecked. As we are protected by God from evil, the vision forces us to consider what our world might be like if God's mercy did not hold back the full destructive powers of sin.

These visions remind us of horrible dreams, unrestrained by conscious reasoning, projecting and expanding our fears to apocalyptic proportions. Like dreams, John's visions describe the wages of sin in terms of nightmarish consequences. The purpose of the succession of trumpet blasts is not to display vengeance, but to provoke interior change in people. God wants to destroy wrongdoing, not wrongdoers. Sadly, people refuse endless opportunities to repent of their idolatry and turn back to God (verse 20). The horrible scenes are a rhetorical work, written in the language of symbolic imagery. The visions are not intended to predict or to accurately describe the future, but to shock the hearers to reject destructive idolatry and to trust in God's power for good.

Reflection and discussion

• Do my nightmares in any way resemble the images associated with the seven trumpets? What do my frightening dreams tell me?

• How have I been stung by the consequences of my own sin? How have I repented and experienced God's mercy?

• What images from our modern era express the horrors of evil? In what way is it true that evil brings its own terrible consequences? 911 ?

Prayer

God of justice and compassion, your anger is just and your mercy unde-served. Deliver me from all evil and shelter me in your presence. Help me to trust that my life and our world are in your hands.

SUGGESTIONS FOR FACILITATORS, GROUP SESSION 3

1. Welcome group members and ask if there are any announcements anyone would like to make.

2. You may want to pray this prayer as a group:

Lord God, you are all holy and almighty, splendidly enthroned at the center of all creation. You are worthy to receive glory and honor and power. Through your Lamb, our Lord and Messiah, you redeemed the world and will bring all creation to its completion. As we experience the greed, terrors, and injustices of our present world, help us remain confident that our victory is assured. As we study the book of Revelation, help us encourage one another with hope and guide us with your Holy Spirit of truth.

3. Ask one or more of the following questions:
   • Which image from the lessons this week stands out most memorably to you?
   • What is the most important lesson you learned through your study this week?

4. Discuss lessons 7 through 12. Choose one or more of the questions for reflection and discussion from each lesson to discuss as a group. You may want to ask group members which question was most challenging or helpful to them as you review each lesson.

5. Remember that there are no definitive answers for these discussion questions. The insights of group members will add to the understanding of all. None of these questions require an expert.

6. After talking about each lesson, instruct group members to complete lessons 13 through 18 on their own during the six days before the next group meeting. They should write out their own answers to the questions as preparation for next week's group discussion.

7. Ask the group if anyone is having any particular problems with the Bible study during the week. You may want to share advice and encouragement within the group.

8. Conclude by praying aloud together the prayer at the end of one of the lessons discussed. You may add to the prayer based on the sharing that has occurred in the group.

So I took the little scroll from the hand of the angel and ate it; it was sweet as honey in my mouth, but when I had eaten it, my stomach was made bitter.

Rev 10:10

The Scroll That Is Bittersweet

REVELATION 10:1–11 ¹*And I saw another mighty angel coming down from heaven, wrapped in a cloud, with a rainbow over his head; his face was like the sun, and his legs like pillars of fire.* ²*He held a little scroll open in his hand. Setting his right foot on the sea and his left foot on the land,* ³*he gave a great shout, like a lion roaring. And when he shouted, the seven thunders sounded.* ⁴*And when the seven thunders had sounded, I was about to write, but I heard a voice from heaven saying, "Seal up what the seven thunders have said, and do not write it down."* ⁵*Then the angel whom I saw standing on the sea and the land*

raised his right hand to heaven

⁶*and swore by him who lives forever and ever,*

who created heaven and what is in it, the earth and what is in it, and the sea and what is in it: "There will be no more delay, ⁷*but in the days when the seventh angel is to blow his trumpet, the mystery of God will be fulfilled, as he announced to his servants the prophets."*

⁸*Then the voice that I had heard from heaven spoke to me again, saying, "Go, take the scroll that is open in the hand of the angel who is standing on the*

sea and on the land." ⁹So I went to the angel and told him to give me the little
scroll; and he said to me, "Take it, and eat; it will be bitter to your stomach, but
sweet as honey in your mouth." ¹⁰So I took the little scroll from the hand of the
angel and ate it; it was sweet as honey in my mouth, but when I had eaten it, my
stomach was made bitter.

¹¹Then they said to me, "You must prophesy again about many peoples and
nations and languages and kings."

Just as there was a delay in the opening of the seventh seal, there is a delay before the seventh and last trumpet blows. Though the kingdom has already been inaugurated in the victory of Christ, there are many delays in the full manifestation of God's reign over all creation. These delays are only from a human point of view, not from God's perspective, for "with the Lord one day is like a thousand years, and a thousand years are like one day" (2 Pet 3:8).

The mighty angel coming from heaven is described as a reflection of God and Christ, whose presence he mediates and whose message he delivers (verses 1–2). His face "like the sun" recalls the opening vision of Christ (1:16). The rainbow mirrors the rainbow around God's heavenly throne (4:3). The "cloud" and "pillars of fire" suggest the guiding presence of God which led Israel through the wilderness. The angel's vast size, bestriding the land and sea, with his right hand raised to heaven, brings together earth, seas, and sky. The message he bears is awesome and is sent from the Creator of "heaven and what is in it, the earth and what is in it, and the sea and what is in it" (verses 5–6).

The sounding of the seven thunders, another series of seven manifestations of judgment, is accompanied by the heavenly command to "seal up what the seven thunders have said, and do not write it down" (verse 4). Thunder, throughout the Old Testament, was described as a manifestation of God's presence. In Psalm 29, the thunder is described seven times as "the voice of the Lord," underlining the strength and majesty of God's voice revealed through a thunderstorm. The sealing of the seven thunders tantalizes us but prevents us from knowing their message. Perhaps this is meant to help us accept the fact that there are some things we cannot know about God's designs. As Jesus said, "But about that day or hour no one knows, neither the angels in heaven, nor the Son, but only the Father" (Mark 13:32).

The scroll that John is told to take and eat, like the scroll with the seven seals, contains God's plan for the world's salvation and the universal extension of his reign. The scroll may be a different way of envisioning the sealed scroll of the earlier vision, just as John's commissioning here may be a different way of looking at his prophetic call from the beginning of the book. The visions of Revelation are not chronological but spiral, continually repeating the same message with different images and different points of view. This scene recalls the prophetic commission of Ezekiel, who is also told to eat the scroll of God's word, as a symbol of his prophetic call (Ezek 3:1–4). As John ingests the word, making God's word his own, the scroll tastes sweet in his mouth, but in his stomach it is bitter (verse 10). The same plan that will win God's victory through Christ also requires suffering and death. God's plan for us is also bittersweet. Though this life is characterized by a mixture of the bitter and the sweet, God's victory for us will bring us joys that last forever.

Reflection and discussion

• In what ways have I experienced God's delays? Are they, in retrospect, beneficial delays for my own ultimate good?

• Is there a bittersweet quality to my life in Christ? How can I consume God's word more completely?

Prayer

> *Father, may your kingdom come. Through the bittersweet experiences of my life, teach me that joy comes through suffering, forgiveness through repentance, and the fullness of life through death.*

The beast that comes up from the bottomless pit will make war on them and conquer them and kill them, and their dead bodies will lie in the street of the great city. Rev 11:7–8

God's Witnesses Are Persecuted by the Beast

REVELATION 11:1–14 *¹Then I was given a measuring rod like a staff, and I was told, "Come and measure the temple of God and the altar and those who worship there, ²but do not measure the court outside the temple; leave that out, for it is given over to the nations, and they will trample over the holy city for forty-two months. ³And I will grant my two witnesses authority to prophesy for one thousand two hundred sixty days, wearing sackcloth."*

⁴These are the two olive trees and the two lampstands that stand before the Lord of the earth. ⁵And if anyone wants to harm them, fire pours from their mouth and consumes their foes; anyone who wants to harm them must be killed in this manner. ⁶They have authority to shut the sky, so that no rain may fall during the days of their prophesying, and they have authority over the waters to turn them into blood, and to strike the earth with every kind of plague, as often as they desire.

⁷When they have finished their testimony, the beast that comes up from the bottomless pit will make war on them and conquer them and kill them, ⁸and their dead bodies will lie in the street of the great city that is prophetically called

Sodom and Egypt, where also their Lord was crucified. ⁹*For three and a half days members of the peoples and tribes and languages and nations will gaze at their dead bodies and refuse to let them be placed in a tomb;* ¹⁰*and the inhabitants of the earth will gloat over them and celebrate and exchange presents, because these two prophets had been a torment to the inhabitants of the earth.*

¹¹*But after the three and a half days, the breath of life from God entered them, and they stood on their feet, and those who saw them were terrified.* ¹²*Then they heard a loud voice from heaven saying to them, "Come up here!" And they went up to heaven in a cloud while their enemies watched them.* ¹³*At that moment there was a great earthquake, and a tenth of the city fell; seven thousand people were killed in the earthquake, and the rest were terrified and gave glory to the God of heaven.*

¹⁴*The second woe has passed. The third woe is coming very soon.*

John's call to measure the temple, the altar, and those who worship within (verse 1) is a continuation of his commission as God's prophet. The gesture is reminiscent of the symbolic actions of the Hebrew prophets (Ezekiel 40). The temple that John measures is not the temple of Jerusalem, which had been destroyed by the Romans, but it is a symbol of the people of God. The measuring serves to protect them from the destructive forces that threaten them with harm, represented by the temple's outer court, which is being trampled over (verse 2). The "forty-two months" during which "the holy city" will be trampled is reminiscent of the three and a half years, or one thousand two hundred and sixty days (verse 3), during which the Seleucid King Antiochus IV seized control over Jerusalem and its temple between 167 and 164 B.C. The three and a half years represents a limited amount of time (half of seven) during which God's people will endure great suffering.

During this painful though limited period, God commissions his people (symbolized by the two witnesses, verse 3) to testify to Jesus Christ and to call society to repentance. They will meet with tremendous opposition by the forces opposed to the reign of God and the Lamb (verses 5–7). God will be with them, not by shielding them from suffering, but by working through them and protecting them until their task is finished. Ultimately God will raise them up victoriously and take them to himself (verses 11–12).

The "two witnesses," representing the people of God, allude to several figures from the Hebrew Scriptures (verses 5–6). Moses, who turned water into blood and struck plagues on the Egyptians with his staff, and Elijah, who called fire from heaven and shut up the skies from raining, are the most obvious reference. The symbols of the olive trees and lampstands (verse 4) allude to Joshua and Zerubbabel, anointed as high priest and king in Jerusalem after the exile (Zech 4). God's people are a priestly and royal people, who serve God and reign with him (1:6; 5:10). The fact that God's people are represented by two witnesses recalls the commission Jesus gave to his disciples as he sent them out in pairs (Luke 10:1). The fact that no one can ultimately harm his witnesses refers to the promise of Jesus: "I have given you authority to tread on snakes and scorpions, and over all the power of the enemy; and nothing will hurt you" (Luke 10:19).

The only "harm" the witnesses do is with their words, symbolized by the consuming fire from their mouth (verse 5). Their persecutors are "torment-ed" by their call to repentance (verse 10). The death, resurrection, and exal-tation of God's witnesses (verses 11–12) repeat the experience of their Lord. They will continue to experience persecution when they are witnesses for Christ, yet they will not be defeated because the power of God will triumph. The fact that a tenth of the city fell should not overshadow the statement that the rest (nine-tenths of the city) repented and gave glory to God as a result of the witness of God's people (verse 13). The message of Revelation remains always a message of hope.

Reflection and discussion

• Do I ever feel that my struggles will go on forever? What does this chapter say to reassure me?

• What indicates that John is not called to measure the physical temple in Jerusalem (verse 1, also 1 Cor 3:16–17)?

• Since the two witnesses represent the vocation of the church throughout time, what pairs of witnesses from the church's history come to mind as examples of this calling?

• Is my life a witness to Christ? What in this chapter gives me courage as a witness?

Prayer

God of life, you raise up people in every age to witness to Christ by suffering in his name. Give me strength and courage when I stand for Christ so that others may come to believe in his message of hope.

Then God's temple in heaven was opened, and the ark of his covenant was seen within his temple; and there were flashes of lightning, rumblings, peals of thunder, an earthquake, and heavy hail. Rev 11:19

The Final Trumpet Sounds

REVELATION 11:15–19 *¹⁵Then the seventh angel blew his trumpet, and there were loud voices in heaven, saying,*

> *"The kingdom of the world has become the kingdom of our Lord*
> *and of his Messiah,*
> *and he will reign forever and ever."*

¹⁶Then the twenty-four elders who sit on their thrones before God fell on their faces and worshiped God, ¹⁷singing,

> *"We give you thanks, Lord God Almighty,*
> *who are and who were,*
> *for you have taken your great power*
> *and begun to reign.*
> *¹⁸The nations raged,*
> *but your wrath has come,*
> *and the time for judging the dead,*
> *for rewarding your servants, the prophets*
> *and saints and all who fear your name,*
> *both small and great,*
> *and for destroying those who destroy the earth."*

¹⁹Then God's temple in heaven was opened, and the ark of his covenant was seen within his temple; and there were flashes of lightning, rumblings, peals of thunder, an earthquake, and heavy hail.

Throughout the Bible, trumpets are blown to summon Israel to battle, to call Israel to repentance, to install new kings, and to convene worshippers for pilgrimage and solemn feasts. God's people associate sounding trumpets with alarm, terror, praise, and joy. The seventh trumpet sounds the final climax of God's triumph over evil and the coming of his kingdom. Instead of more plagues and woes, we are surprised to hear an outburst of rejoicing in heaven. It is a victory celebration: "The kingdom of the world has become the kingdom of our Lord and of his Messiah, and he will reign forever and ever" (verse 15).

The twenty-four elders then sing of how God's reign has now been established. It is time for the dead to be judged and for the faithful to be rewarded (verses 17–18). The victory of God over evil has been won. As seen from the viewpoint of eternity, God's purposes are already fulfilled in the triumph of Christ on the cross. The kingdom of the world has indeed become the kingdom of God where he will reign with the Lamb forever. The heavenly scene reflects the inner reality and final outcome of earthly events. The ultimate goal of the first six seals and trumpets is not destruction but the liberation of all humanity and the whole earth from oppressive and destructive powers. This is the hope that John's vision places before us.

As all of heaven gives thanks, God's temple in heaven opens and the ark of the covenant—the sign of God's covenant that once only the high priest could see—could be seen by all God's people. The sight of the ark means that the holy of holies, where the ark once stood, is open to all. The gospels tell us that at the death of Jesus, the veil of the temple was torn in two (Mark 15:38). This was the veil in front of the holy of holies, the sacred dwelling place of God. The same reality is expressed here in Revelation: access to God is now possible for all people. By his death on the cross, Jesus triumphed once and for all over sin and death. The result is that victory is displayed here as a vision of heaven and the open temple of God—perfect access to God and a clear vision of his splendor.

If John had finished his book here, we would have considered it properly terminated. The victory is won and God's purposes have been accomplished.

But the opening of God's temple in heaven becomes the prelude to even more wondrous visions: a woman clothed with the sun and a great red dragon. Clearly there is much more to be revealed.

Reflection and discussion

• How does the seventh trumpet reveal the purposes of the first six trumpets?

• In what way is the revelation of the holy of holies and the ark of the covenant in heaven an expression of Christ's victorious death on the cross?

• In the midst of life's problems, do I believe that Christ reigns over the world and promises me victory?

Prayer

Victorious Lord, I give you thanks for your cross which has redeemed the world. Through your saving death all people can worship you and experience the divine presence. Reign over my life and give me joy in worshiping you.

She gave birth to a son, a male child, who is to rule all the nations with a rod of iron. But her child was snatched away and taken to God and to his throne; and the woman fled into the wilderness. Rev 12:5–6

The Glorious Woman and the Great Red Dragon

REVELATION 12:1–17 *¹A great portent appeared in heaven: a woman clothed with the sun, with the moon under her feet, and on her head a crown of twelve stars. ²She was pregnant and was crying out in birthpangs, in the agony of giving birth. ³Then another portent appeared in heaven: a great red dragon, with seven heads and ten horns, and seven diadems on his heads. ⁴His tail swept down a third of the stars of heaven and threw them to the earth. Then the dragon stood before the woman who was about to bear a child, so that he might devour her child as soon as it was born. ⁵And she gave birth to a son, a male child, who is to rule all the nations with a rod of iron. But her child was snatched away and taken to God and to his throne; ⁶and the woman fled into the wilderness, where she has a place prepared by God, so that there she can be nourished for one thousand two hundred sixty days.*

⁷And war broke out in heaven; Michael and his angels fought against the dragon. The dragon and his angels fought back, ⁸but they were defeated, and there was no longer any place for them in heaven. ⁹The great dragon was thrown down, that ancient serpent, who is called the Devil and Satan, the deceiver of the whole world—he was thrown down to the earth, and his angels were thrown down with him.

¹⁰ *Then I heard a loud voice in heaven, proclaiming,*
"Now have come the salvation and the power
   and the kingdom of our God
   and the authority of his Messiah,
for the accuser of our comrades has been thrown down,
   who accuses them day and night before our God.
¹¹ *But they have conquered him by the blood of the Lamb*
   and by the word of their testimony,
for they did not cling to life even in the face of death.
¹² *Rejoice then, you heavens*
   and those who dwell in them!
But woe to the earth and the sea,
   for the devil has come down to you
with great wrath,
   because he knows that his time is short!"

¹³ *So when the dragon saw that he had been thrown down to the earth, he pursued the woman who had given birth to the male child.* ¹⁴ *But the woman was given the two wings of the great eagle, so that she could fly from the serpent into the wilderness, to her place where she is nourished for a time, and times, and half a time.* ¹⁵ *Then from his mouth the serpent poured water like a river after the woman, to sweep her away with the flood.* ¹⁶ *But the earth came to the help of the woman; it opened its mouth and swallowed the river that the dragon had poured from his mouth.* ¹⁷ *Then the dragon was angry with the woman, and went off to make war on the rest of her children, those who keep the commandments of God and hold the testimony of Jesus.*

As God's temple in heaven opened, displaying the holy of holies and the ark of the covenant (11:19), what was previously hidden is now revealed to all. In the heavens "a great portent" appears, marking the beginning of a new series of visions. John sees "a woman clothed with the sun, with the moon under her feet, and on her head a crown of twelve stars" (verse 1). She is pregnant and crying out in birth pangs (verse 2). Meanwhile, John sees an ominous portent, "a great red dragon, with seven heads and ten horns" standing before the woman in order to devour her child as soon as it is born. The woman bears a son, but the child is saved from the dragon by God's intervention (verses 3–5).

The image of the queen of heaven with the divine child was internationally known in the mythology of Babylonia, Egypt, Greece, and Asia Minor. In Egyptian lore, the goddess Isis gives birth to the sun god Horus while being pursued by the red dragon Set who swallows the sun each night. In the Greek tradition, the mother of Apollo is pursued by the dragon Python, but is given refuge on the island of Delos where Apollo is born. Apollo, the sun god, eventually slays the dragon. In Asia Minor of John's day, the queen of heaven was the goddess Roma, the mother of the gods. Her child was the Roman emperor, an incarnation of the sun god Apollo, celebrated as the world's lord and savior.

The pains of giving birth associate the woman with the people of Israel awaiting the delivery of the messianic age (Isa 26:17; 66:7–9; Mic 4:9–10). The twelve stars on her head are the twelve tribes of Israel. The prophets commonly portrayed the enemies of Israel under the figure of the dragon or serpent (Isa 27:1). Within this symbolic context, the dragon represents the ultimate foe of God's people. The woman's escape into the wilderness alludes to Israel's journey through the desert where God's people are nourished and protected. The enmity between the serpent and the woman recalls the primeval story in the creation accounts in which Eve is pursued in the garden. The result was a lasting conflict between the woman's offspring and the serpent, the ultimate result of which is the crushing of the serpent's head (Gen 3:15).

Clearly the vision of the woman, her child, and the dragon has multiple layers of meaning. The woman is the personification of ancient Israel giving birth to its messiah. On the historical level, the image refers to Mary, the daughter of Israel, who gave birth to Israel's messiah. The dragon's eagerness to devour the child expresses the violent opposition that Jesus met during his earthly life, beginning with Herod's slaughter of the children at his birth (Matt 2:16) and continuing to his crucifixion. The woman is also the personification of Christ's church, the persecuted followers of Christ continually pursued by the foes of God's people. Mary, as mother of Christ's disciples, also represents the church as it continually brings Christ to birth in the world under the threat of persecution. The dragon represents all those forces of evil that seek to destroy Christ and his church. While Christ was taken up to the throne of God, his church continues to experience the threat of suffering and persecution for a limited period of time (verses 5–6).

Revelation gives us a two-level view of reality. On earth the church experiences continual opposition and the outcome seems uncertain. Yet, when we look to heaven, we see a cosmic battle between the forces of good and evil, the powers of God and the forces of darkness. The outcome is clear: the dragon is beaten, the powers of Satan are vanquished. The heavenly vision hammers this truth home, saying that he is "defeated" (verse 8), "thrown down" (verses 9–10), and "conquered" (verse 11). Michael is the guardian and defender of God's people in the Hebrew Scriptures. His defeat of the dragon represents the victory won by "the blood of the Lamb," the atoning death of Christ, and the witness of his followers (verse 11).

Though defeated, the dragon remains on the scene. Cast down from heaven, he turns his fury on the woman and the rest of her children, the followers of Christ on earth (verses 13, 17). This is the present situation of John and his community, the state of the oppressed people of God. The eagle's wings that sweep the woman to safety are an image of God's protective care (verse 14; Exod 19:4; Deut 32:11). Though evil remains powerful, we have the assurance of protection and victory through the power of our God.

Reflection and discussion

• How is the life of the church a continuation of the opposition Christ faced throughout his life? How is my own life a spiritual battle?

• How do we participate in the Lamb's conquest of the powers of the dragon (verse 11)?

• In what way does the glorious woman represent both Mary and the church?

• How have I experienced God lifting me up on eagles' wings (verse 14), protecting me in times of trial?

• What is the most hopeful message of this scene for me?

Prayer

Lord God, help me to see my suffering in light of the suffering of Christ and of your people through the ages. I know that the blood of the Lamb has conquered the powers of evil. Strengthen your church as we await the return of your Son.

It was allowed to make war on the saints and to conquer them. It was given authority over every tribe and people and language and nation, and all the inhabitants of the earth will worship it. Rev 12:7–8

The Beast Rising From the Sea

REVELATION 12:18—13:10 ¹⁸*Then the dragon took his stand on the sand of the seashore. ¹And I saw a beast rising out of the sea having ten horns and seven heads; and on its horns were ten diadems, and on its heads were blasphemous names. ²And the beast that I saw was like a leopard, its feet were like a bear's, and its mouth was like a lion's mouth. And the dragon gave it his power and his throne and great authority. ³One of its heads seemed to have received a death-blow, but its mortal wound had been healed. In amazement the whole earth followed the beast. ⁴They worshiped the dragon, for he had given his authority to the beast, and they worshiped the beast, saying, "Who is like the beast, and who can fight against it?"*

⁵The beast was given a mouth uttering haughty and blasphemous words, and it was allowed to exercise authority for forty-two months. ⁶It opened its mouth to utter blasphemies against God, blaspheming his name and his dwelling, that is, those who dwell in heaven. ⁷Also it was allowed to make war on the saints and to conquer them. It was given authority over every tribe and people and language and nation, ⁸and all the inhabitants of the earth will worship

*it, everyone whose name has not been written from the foundation of the world
in the book of life of the Lamb that was slaughtered.*
   ⁹Let anyone who has an ear listen:
   ¹⁰If you are to be taken captive,
      into captivity you go;
   if you kill with the sword,
      with the sword you must be killed.
Here is a call for the endurance and faith of the saints.

As the dragon stands on the seashore and gathers allies for his war on the children of the heavenly woman, two beasts rise up, one from the sea and one from the land. Both derive their authority and power from the dragon and serve as his agents. The beast from the sea looks like the dragon, with seven heads and ten horns (verse 1, compared to 12:3). It is further described as a composite animal, with leopard, bear, and lion parts. The features of the beasts are derived from the book of Daniel, in which four beasts represent four world empires that made war on Israel (Dan 7). Combining the features of Daniel's four beasts, the beast from the sea represents total dehumanizing power and oppressive rule.

The beast is depicted as a parody of the Lamb. The beast shares the throne of the dragon (verse 2); the Lamb shares the throne of God. One of the beast's heads seemed to have received a death blow, but its mortal wound had been healed (verse 3). A similar description has been given of the Lamb who had been slain yet now lives. Moreover, the blasphemous names of the beast parody the names of Christ given throughout the work: Word of God, King of kings, and Lord of lords. Just as followers of the Lamb come from all nations, tongues, and peoples, the beast is given authority over "every tribe and people and language and nation" (verse 7) and all the inhabitants of the earth worship it (verse 8). The rhetoric of Revelation is uncompromising: one must decide either for God or for Satan, for the Lamb or for the beast.

Though the image of the beast can represent any power that demands the place of God in people's lives, at the time of John the description of the beast called to mind the authority of the Roman empire. These parts of the description make the reference almost certain: the whole world followed the beast (verse 3); nothing can compare with it or fight against it (verse 4); and it waged war against the followers of Christ (verse 7). The Roman emperors were given divine status and worshiped by the people. Temples were built to their honor, mocking the dwelling place of God, and they were given titles that belonged to God alone: savior, lord, and god. Clearly John is writing about events that were taking place as he wrote, not events in the distant future. Christians who refused to take part in the rituals of imperial worship were persecuted, imprisoned, and killed (verse 10). The followers of Christ were called to loyal resistance and faithful steadfastness.

While the Roman empire disappeared centuries ago, the beast of John's vision remains very much alive. Wealth, position, and military strength are too often seen as sources of real power and authority. The cry of those who worship the beast did not cease with the fall of Rome. It echoes in every heart that refuses to acknowledge the reign of God and the Lamb.

Reflection and discussion

• In what ways is the beast from the sea a mockery of the Lamb?

• Do I offer total devotion to God or do I compromise my allegiance in some ways? What human powers usurp the place of God in my life?

Prayer

Lord Jesus, help me to make you the only Lord of my life. Strengthen me when I am tempted to prefer my will over yours, and when I trust my power more than yours.

Let anyone with understanding calculate the number of the beast, for it is the number of a person. Its number is six hundred sixty-six. Rev 13:18

The Beast Rising From the Earth

REVELATION 13:11–18 *¹¹Then I saw another beast that rose out of the earth; it had two horns like a lamb and it spoke like a dragon. ¹²It exercises all the authority of the first beast on its behalf, and it makes the earth and its inhabitants worship the first beast, whose mortal wound had been healed. ¹³It performs great signs, even making fire come down from heaven to earth in the sight of all; ¹⁴and by the signs that it is allowed to perform on behalf of the beast, it deceives the inhabitants of earth, telling them to make an image for the beast that had been wounded by the sword and yet lived; ¹⁵and it was allowed to give breath to the image of the beast so that the image of the beast could even speak and cause those who would not worship the image of the beast to be killed. ¹⁶Also it causes all, both small and great, both rich and poor, both free and slave, to be marked on the right hand or the forehead, ¹⁷so that no one can buy or sell who does not have the mark, that is, the name of the beast or the number of its name. ¹⁸This calls for wisdom: let anyone with understanding calculate the number of the beast, for it is the number of a person. Its number is six hundred sixty-six.*

The beast that rose out of the earth looks like the Lamb, but the resemblance is clearly superficial. It has horns like a lamb, thus exercising the power of the Lamb, but it speaks the language of the dragon, doing its bidding (verse 11). Deceptively imitating the Lamb, it tries to imitate the worship of the true God. But in reality it entices people to the false religion of the dragon. Clearly we have here a wolf in lamb's clothing (Matt 7:15). This second beast symbolizes the false religion of the empire that promotes emperor worship. It activates the authority of the first beast and seeks to persuade the whole world to worship it. As the Lamb has invited people from throughout the earth to become a kingdom and priests serving God (5:10), the beast seeks to mislead the whole world into becoming a cultic community of the dragon who worship the first beast (verse 12).

The mark which the beast forces all people to bear (verse 16) is the seal of the emperor. Slaves could be branded with the seal of their owners on their forehead or hands. As slaves of the emperor, people who worship him are said to be marked with the number 666 (verse 18). This mark of the beast is a distorted imitation of the protective seal placed on the forehead of God's people (7:2–3). The meaning of the number must have been well known to Revelation's original audience, but it is no longer known to us. Since the author stresses that the number stands for a human figure, scholars have suggested numerous people represented by this number. The most common suggestion is that it represents the emperor Nero. In Hebrew, which used letters instead of numbers for counting, the numerical value of his name and title, "Caesar Nero," totals 666. As the first emperor to launch a Roman persecution of Christians, Nero seems a logical choice to represent the Roman regime, which attempts to put itself in the position of God.

The dragon shares its power and authority with the two beasts. In this "counterfeit trinity" of the dragon and the two beasts, the beast from the earth is a mockery of the Holy Spirit. Its purpose is to make the inhabitants of the earth worship the first beast, the Roman empire (verse 12), even as God's Spirit invites people to worship Christ. It performs great signs, mocking the miracles and wonders the disciples of Jesus were able to perform through the Spirit working within them. The beast even makes "fire come down from heaven" (verse 13), a parody of the Pentecostal flames of God's true Spirit. Its chief characteristic is deception, "it deceives the inhabitants of the earth" (verse 14), a cruel parody of Christ's promise to send the "Spirit of truth" who will guide disciples into all the truth (John 16:13). The mark of the beast (verse 17) is the final mockery of God's true Spirit. The beast forces the people of the earth to receive the seal of the beast, whereas those who hear the word of truth, the gospel of salvation, are "marked with the seal of the promised Holy Spirit" (Eph 1:13).

Like the first beast, this second beast and its mark continues to influence people down to our day. Revelation's depiction of ultimate evil penetrating the structures of society and political and economic governance can best be understood today as systemic evil and structural sin. Those who refuse to follow it are threatened with oppression and economic devastation. Revelation consistently speaks of the satanic powers of evil in political, economic, national, and cosmic terms. The influence of the dragon that has been cast down to the earth and the power of the beasts is alive today. The choice between the Lamb and the beasts is just as clear today as it was for the churches of Asia Minor.

Reflection and discussion

• In what way is the beast from the earth a mockery of the Holy Spirit?

• What are the structural sins that infiltrate national, political, and economic systems today?

• For what reasons are the dragon and the two beasts called a "counterfeit trinity"?

• How can making the sign of the cross in faith protect me from the deceptions of the beasts?

• How do I react to people who use these visions to present a timetable for events in our day? In what ways does the struggle between the followers of the beast and the Lamb continue today?

Prayer

Father, Son, and Holy Spirit, fill my mind with your truth when I encounter deception. Reinforce my heart with love when I confront hatred. Fill me with hope with I am tempted to despair.

SUGGESTIONS FOR FACILITATORS, GROUP SESSION 4

1. Welcome group members and ask if anyone has any questions, announcements, or requests.

2. You may want to pray this prayer as a group:

Lord God, we know that our world is influenced by the dragon and its deceptive beasts, the forces opposed to your reign of justice and peace. Send us your Spirit of truth and protect us from deception and evil. Lift us up as on wings of an eagle, so that we may be assured of your ultimate victory. As we gather as your people, give us a deep desire to consume your word, and make us witnesses to Christ by what we say and do.

3. Ask one or more of the following questions:
   • What is the most difficult part of this study for you?
   • What insights stands out to you from the lessons this week?

4. Discuss lessons 13 through 18. Choose one or more of the questions for reflection and discussion from each lesson to discuss as a group. You may want to ask group members which question was most challenging or helpful to them as you review each lesson.

5. Keep the discussion moving, but allow time for the questions that provoke the most discussion. Encourage the group members to use "I" language in their responses.

6. After talking over each lesson, instruct group members to complete lessons 19 through 24 on their own during the six days before the next group meeting. They should write out their own answers to the questions as preparation for next week's session.

7. Ask the group what encouragement they need for the coming week. Ask the members to pray for the needs of one another during the week.

8. Conclude by praying aloud together the prayer at the end of one of the lessons discussed. You may choose to conclude the prayer by asking members to pray aloud any requests they may have.

Then I looked, and there was the Lamb, standing on Mount Zion! And with him were one hundred forty-four thousand who had his name and his Father's name written on their foreheads. Rev 14:1

Worship and Follow the Lamb

REVELATION 14:1–13 *¹Then I looked, and there was the Lamb, standing on Mount Zion! And with him were one hundred forty-four thousand who had his name and his Father's name written on their foreheads. ²And I heard a voice from heaven like the sound of many waters and like the sound of loud thunder; the voice I heard was like the sound of harpists playing on their harps, ³and they sing a new song before the throne and before the four living creatures and before the elders. No one could learn that song except the one hundred forty-four thousand who have been redeemed from the earth. ⁴It is these who have not defiled themselves with women, for they are virgins; these follow the Lamb wherever he goes. They have been redeemed from humankind as first fruits for God and the Lamb, ⁵and in their mouth no lie was found; they are blameless.*

⁶Then I saw another angel flying in midheaven, with an eternal gospel to proclaim to those who live on the earth—to every nation and tribe and language and people. ⁷He said in a loud voice, "Fear God and give him glory, for the hour of his judgment has come; and worship him who made heaven and earth, the sea and the springs of water."

⁸*Then another angel, a second, followed, saying, "Fallen, fallen is Babylon the great! She has made all nations drink of the wine of the wrath of her fornication."*

⁹*Then another angel, a third, followed them, crying with a loud voice, "Those who worship the beast and its image, and receive a mark on their foreheads or on their hands,* ¹⁰*they will also drink the wine of God's wrath, poured unmixed into the cup of his anger, and they will be tormented with fire and sulfur in the presence of the holy angels and in the presence of the Lamb.* ¹¹*And the smoke of their torment goes up forever and ever. There is no rest day or night for those who worship the beast and its image and for anyone who receives the mark of its name."*

¹²*Here is a call for the endurance of the saints, those who keep the commandments of God and hold fast to the faith of Jesus.*

¹³*And I heard a voice from heaven saying, "Write this: Blessed are the dead who from now on die in the Lord." "Yes," says the Spirit, "they will rest from their labors, for their deeds follow them."*

The Lamb standing on Mount Zion forms a strong contrast with the beasts from the sea and the land. The 144,000 who bear the names of the Lamb and the Father on their foreheads form the antithesis of those who bear the name and number of the beast (verse 1; 13:16–18). These are the 144,000 of chapter 7, the twelve thousand from each of the twelve tribes of the restored Israel. The scene is one of worship and rejoicing. John often alternates between scenes of horror and scenes of consolation. The sound that John hears comes from heaven. It is compared to rushing water, pealing thunder, and the music of harps—combining images of power and gentleness (verse 2). The new song sung before God's throne celebrates God's redeeming act, the Lamb's triumph and God's judgment of the earth. Only the 144,000—those "who have been redeemed from the earth"—are able to learn the hymn.

The 144,000 symbolize the faithful witnesses to the Lamb: "they follow the Lamb wherever he goes" (verse 4). They are described as male virgins, evoking the imagery of holy war in which participants must remain ritually pure by abstaining from sexual activity. Yet, like the Lamb, this holy army will win the war with the beast not with violence but with faithfulness. They are called "blameless" (verse 5), literally "without blemish." In union with the unblemished sacrificial Lamb, they will conquer through their faithful witness and sacrificial death. The mention of sexual purity also recalls the language of the Hebrew prophets in which participation in pagan worship was called "fornication" or "adultery," infidelity to God. This signifies that the 144,000 are those who have not taken part in the worship of the beast, but have remained faithful to the Lamb.

This vision of the Lamb and his faithful witnesses is followed by the appearance of three angels acting as heavenly messengers. The first message is announced as an "eternal gospel" and insists on the worship of God alone (verse 6). Surely this is the heart of the conflict: who and how one ought to worship. The second angel announces the fall of Babylon (verse 8), a preview of the scenes of judgment that will come. "The wine of the wrath of her fornications" describes her seductive power over all the people of the Roman empire. The third angel contrasts the triumphant scene of the Lamb on Mount Zion with the condemnation of those who worship the beast and receive its mark (verses 9–11).

The purpose of the visions is to call God's people to "endurance," to help them hold fast to their faith in the midst of the trials of the present time (verse 12). The voice from heaven offers assurance to those who battle in the Lamb's army: "Blessed are the dead who from now on die in the Lord" (verse 13). Their death will be "rest from their labors" and their good works will be witnesses for them before the just Judge.

Reflection and discussion

• How is the army of the Lamb a force of nonviolent love? How do the Lamb and his followers conquer without aggression and violence?

• Why do people sometimes wear external marks to express their identity, beliefs, or commitments?

• In what way can virginity and celibacy symbolize commitment and faithfulness? In what way can marriage express the same?

• How does my reflection on the end of earthly life affect my attitude about daily life (verse 13)?

Prayer

Victorious Lamb, you call me to follow you wherever you go. I long for the day when you will come with salvation for all your people. Give me the strength and courage to remain faithful to you now and forever.

"Use your sickle and reap, for the hour to reap has come, because the harvest of the earth is fully ripe." Rev 14:15

Harvesting the Grain and the Grapes

REVELATION 14:14–20 *¹⁴Then I looked, and there was a white cloud, and seated on the cloud was one like the Son of Man, with a golden crown on his head, and a sharp sickle in his hand! ¹⁵Another angel came out of the temple, calling with a loud voice to the one who sat on the cloud, "Use your sickle and reap, for the hour to reap has come, because the harvest of the earth is fully ripe." ¹⁶So the one who sat on the cloud swung his sickle over the earth, and the earth was reaped.*

¹⁷Then another angel came out of the temple in heaven, and he too had a sharp sickle. ¹⁸Then another angel came out from the altar, the angel who has authority over fire, and he called with a loud voice to him who had the sharp sickle, "Use your sharp sickle and gather the clusters of the vine of the earth, for its grapes are ripe." ¹⁹So the angel swung his sickle over the earth and gathered the vintage of the earth, and he threw it into the great wine press of the wrath of God. ²⁰And the wine press was trodden outside the city, and blood flowed from the wine press, as high as a horse's bridle, for a distance of about two hundred miles.

The Son of Man, the harvest master of the final judgment, is described using the now familiar symbolism from Daniel 7 of the majestic human coming on the clouds. The Son of Man evokes the inaugural vision (1:13) and surely represents the glorified Christ. The gold crown of victory now replaces his crown of thorns. He holds a sickle and is ready for the harvest. The parables of Jesus contain similar images of the time of judgment: "The harvest is the end of the age, and the reapers are angels" (Matt 13:39). Paralleling the grain harvest (verses 14–16) with the grape harvest (verses 17–20) evokes the bread and wine associated with the Eucharist, an anticipation of final glory and the unity of all the faithful with Christ.

The signal to reap the harvest reflects the words of the prophet Joel: "Put in the sickle, for the harvest is ripe. Go in, tread, for the wine press is full. The vats overflow, for their wickedness is great" (Joel 3:13). The great bloodbath is the blood of the martyrs as well as the blood of those opposed to God's reign. The winepress is trodden "outside the city" (verse 20), the place where the blood of Christ was shed on the cross (Heb 13:12). His bloody victory anticipates the victory of his followers. Like Christ, they are rejected by the worldly city. His death was God's judgment: "Now is the judgment of this world; now the ruler of this world will be driven out" (John 12:31). The flowing blood represents both suffering and life. The blood that flows from the winepress, like the blood of Jesus, covers the whole earth.

We cannot understand John's bloody rhetoric if we interpret it as a prediction of inevitable events rather than an evocative warning eliciting repentance. The message is that God is just, not that God is vengeful. Even this message, however, must be balanced with the teaching of Jesus that God is merciful, showering good even on those who do evil (Matt 5:43–45). It is nevertheless sobering to realize that the dreadful metaphors of these verses fall short of describing the eternal violence we can do to ourselves by separating ourselves from God and his saving will for us.

Reflection and discussion

• What is the difference between the two types of harvest presented in this vision?

• How ready is the world for harvest? How ripe is my life for the reaping?

• What message do these verses convey to me about the justice of God?

Prayer

Lord of the harvest, you are a God of perfect justice as well as overwhelming mercy. Gather me to yourself in your final harvest of the earth. Save me from my sin and never let me be separated from you.

I saw what appeared to be a sea of glass mixed with fire, and those who had conquered the beast and its image and the number of its name, standing beside the sea of glass with harps of God in their hands. Rev 15:2

The Song of the Lamb

REVELATION 15:1–8 ¹*Then I saw another portent in heaven, great and amazing: seven angels with seven plagues, which are the last, for with them the wrath of God is ended.*

²*And I saw what appeared to be a sea of glass mixed with fire, and those who had conquered the beast and its image and the number of its name, standing beside the sea of glass with harps of God in their hands.* ³*And they sing the song of Moses, the servant of God, and the song of the Lamb:*

"Great and amazing are your deeds,
 Lord God the Almighty!
Just and true are your ways,
 King of the nations!
⁴*Lord, who will not fear*
 and glorify your name?
For you alone are holy.
 All nations will come
 and worship before you,
for your judgments have been revealed."
⁵*After this I looked, and the temple of the tent of witness in heaven was*

opened, ⁶and out of the temple came the seven angels with the seven plagues, robed in pure bright linen, with golden sashes across their chests. ⁷Then one of the four living creatures gave the seven angels seven golden bowls full of the wrath of God, who lives forever and ever; ⁸and the temple was filled with smoke from the glory of God and from his power, and no one could enter the temple until the seven plagues of the seven angels were ended.

Before narrating the seven plagues of God's wrath, anticipated by the seven angels holding the seven bowls (verses 1, 6–8), John gives us another image of security and salvation. "Those who had conquered the beast and its image and the number of its name" were celebrating their deliverance from God's wrath (verse 2). With harps in hand they sang both the song of Moses (Exod 15:1–8)—Israel's song of victory over their Egyptian oppressors—and the song of the Lamb (verses 3–4)—the new song of God's victory over the power of their persecutors. In the Exodus, God's people crossed over the sea, leaving their oppressors behind. Now, having passed through suffering, God's people stand on a "sea of glass." This new exodus leads to the promised land of God's presence where God's people can sing the song of victory.

This song of the Lamb, like the other hymns of Revelation, was probably sung in the liturgy of the early church. Indeed God's deeds are "great and amazing." God's ways are "just and true." The song asks how anyone could fail to fear or glorify the all-holy God, and looks to all the nations to acknowledge and worship him. He is the true and only "King of the nations." This heavenly song is given to us now on earth as an encouragement to trust in God despite the temporary sufferings of our lives. When we pray with the angels and saints, we anticipate the life that will be ours.

The seven angels with the seven plagues come forth from the heavenly temple, dressed much like the risen Christ in the book's opening vision (1:13). Their bright linen garments and golden sashes indicate that they serve the Lamb and share in his victory. The exodus imagery of the song of Moses and the sea of glass anticipates the seven plagues of the coming visions, which are strongly influenced by the events associated with the exodus of ancient Israel. John always gives us a heavenly vision before bringing us back to the earthy level of persecution and disaster. Unlike our ancestors who had to endure slavery before crossing the sea and singing the song of Moses, we are able to anticipate victory and sing the song of the Lamb before our earthly trial is over.

Reflection and discussion

• How is the song of Moses similar to the song of the Lamb? Why are they sung together by those who conquer?

• Why does John offer us this heavenly scene of victory and song before narrating the seven plagues upon the earth? How does the viewpoint of heaven help me understand the reality of the earth?

• What are some other "great and amazing" deeds of God? In what way are his ways "just and true"?

Prayer

O King of the nations, you alone are holy. Your deeds are great and amazing; your ways are just and true. In every age you deliver your people from bondage and oppression. Bring me to freedom and let me experience the fullness of your salvation.

The great city was split into three parts, and the cities of the nations fell. God remembered great Babylon and gave her the wine-cup of the fury of his **wrath.** Rev 16:19

Seven Bowls of God's Wrath

REVELATION 16:1–21 ¹*Then I heard a loud voice from the temple telling the seven angels, "Go and pour out on the earth the seven bowls of the wrath of God."*

²So the first angel went and poured his bowl on the earth, and a foul and painful sore came on those who had the mark of the beast and who worshiped its image.

³The second angel poured his bowl into the sea, and it became like the blood of a corpse, and every living thing in the sea died.

⁴The third angel poured his bowl into the rivers and the springs of water, and they became blood. ⁵And I heard the angel of the waters say,

"You are just, O Holy One, who are and were,
*   for you have judged these things;*
⁶because they shed the blood of saints and prophets,
*   you have given them blood to drink.*
It is what they deserve!"

[7]*And I heard the altar respond,*

"Yes, O Lord God, the Almighty,

your judgments are true and just!"

[8]*The fourth angel poured his bowl on the sun, and it was allowed to scorch them with fire;* [9]*they were scorched by the fierce heat, but they cursed the name of God, who had authority over these plagues, and they did not repent and give him glory.*

[10]*The fifth angel poured his bowl on the throne of the beast, and its kingdom was plunged into darkness; people gnawed their tongues in agony,* [11]*and cursed the God of heaven because of their pains and sores, and they did not repent of their deeds.*

[12]*The sixth angel poured his bowl on the great river Euphrates, and its water was dried up in order to prepare the way for the kings from the east.* [13]*And I saw three foul spirits like frogs coming from the mouth of the dragon, from the mouth of the beast, and from the mouth of the false prophet.* [14]*These are demonic spirits, performing signs, who go abroad to the kings of the whole world, to assemble them for battle on the great day of God the Almighty.* [15]*("See, I am coming like a thief! Blessed is the one who stays awake and is clothed, not going about naked and exposed to shame.")* [16]*And they assembled them at the place that in Hebrew is called Harmagedon.*

[17]*The seventh angel poured his bowl into the air, and a loud voice came out of the temple, from the throne, saying, "It is done!"* [18]*And there came flashes of lightning, rumblings, peals of thunder, and a violent earthquake, such as had not occurred since people were upon the earth, so violent was that earthquake.* [19]*The great city was split into three parts, and the cities of the nations fell. God remembered great Babylon and gave her the wine-cup of the fury of his wrath.* [20]*And every island fled away, and no mountains were to be found;* [21]*and huge hailstones, each weighing about a hundred pounds, dropped from heaven on people, until they cursed God for the plague of the hail, so fearful was that plague.*

Revelation continually spirals back on itself, repeating its basic message with new images. We have seen calamities associated with the opening of the seven seals and the blowing of the seven trumpets. Now John describes another series of tribulations, symbolized by the pouring out of the contents of seven bowls. Again, the imagery is taken from the series of plagues which struck Egypt at the time of the exodus (sores, water turned to blood, darkness, frogs, hail—see Exod 7–10). Yet here the destruction is intensified to an almost unimaginable degree. The seven bowls of wrath are poured consecutively on the earth, on the sea, on the rivers and springs, on the sun, on the throne of the beast, on the Euphrates River, and finally into the air. The disasters are even worse than the tribulations associated with the seven seals and the seven trumpets. Whereas previously only a fourth or a third of the earth was struck, the effects of these plagues are universal.

John presents us with scenes of intense terror, yet their purpose, like the plagues of Egypt, is to turn people away from their rejection of God. Yet, like Pharaoh in the exodus, the people did not repent and give God glory, but instead they continued to curse God (verse 9, 11). At the end, they go on cursing God; no repentance is mentioned (verse 21). After repeated refusals of God's invitations, people's rejection of his grace can become final.

While the images used to describe the consequences of God's justice are harsh, God is not presented as cruel or vengeful. God's judgment is described as the working out of his justice upon those who turn from him and worship the beast. John makes it clear that those who experience the plagues receive the consequences of their own actions. Because they shed the blood of the saints and prophets, they have been given blood to drink (verse 6). As the third angel proclaims, "It is what they deserve." John presents these terrors so that people can see the consequences of their actions so that they can repent and experience the fullness of life. By speaking of the "wrath of God," John uses a human emotional response to symbolize God's unrelenting opposition to sin. When God manifests his presence in the world, his appearance brings delight to some and horror to others. But God is not two-faced; God has only the face of love. But the face seems terrible to those who have committed their lives against him.

The last three plagues describe the destruction of the beast and the end of its reign: the throne of the beast is destroyed (verse 10), its empire is invaded (verses 12–16), and its capital city is demolished (verse 19). Three demonic spirits like frogs come from the mouths of the "counterfeit trinity" (verse 13), the dragon, the first beast, and the false prophet (the second beast). They lead the kings of the earth to the place of the great battle, Harmagedon (verse 16). Attempts to locate Harmagedon at Megiddo or other places in the Holy Land are futile. Its significance is not geographic, but symbolic. It represents the last resistance of the demonic forces of the beasts before the full realization of Christ's reign. John is not speculating about the location of some future military battle; rather he is characterizing the suddenness and surety of God's eventual victory over the forces of evil.

Pain, as C.S. Lewis once put it, is God's megaphone for getting through to us when quieter words are ignored. Pain shows us our need for God and helps us see the insufficiency of the idols on which we rely rather than on him. John is brutally honest about suffering. Our modern times provide images of evil's horror: mass graves filled with corpses, mushroom clouds over radiated cities, emaciated children dying of hunger, pools of blood left by suicide bombers. These images seem just as horrid as the seven bowls. Evil brings its own terrible consequences.

Reflection and discussion

• What do the sayings of 13:10 and 16:6 say to me about God's justice? In what way does the principle, "we get what we deserve" (16:6), help me understand the seven plagues?

• In what way has pain been God's megaphone for me?

Prayer

O my God, I am truly sorry for having offended you. I detest all my sins because of your just punishments. Be merciful to me in your judgments and let me experience your forgiveness.

They will make war on the Lamb, and the Lamb will conquer them, for he is Lord of lords and King of kings, and those with him are called and chosen and faithful. Rev 17:14

The Great Harlot Who Rides the Beast

REVELATION 17:1–18 *¹Then one of the seven angels who had the seven bowls came and said to me, "Come, I will show you the judgment of the great whore who is seated on many waters, ²with whom the kings of the earth have committed fornication, and with the wine of whose fornication the inhabitants of the earth have become drunk." ³So he carried me away in the spirit into a wilderness, and I saw a woman sitting on a scarlet beast that was full of blasphemous names, and it had seven heads and ten horns. ⁴The woman was clothed in purple and scarlet, and adorned with gold and jewels and pearls, holding in her hand a golden cup full of abominations and the impurities of her fornication; ⁵and on her forehead was written a name, a mystery: "Babylon the great, mother of whores and of earth's abominations." ⁶And I saw that the woman was drunk with the blood of the saints and the blood of the witnesses to Jesus.*

When I saw her, I was greatly amazed. ⁷But the angel said to me, "Why are you so amazed? I will tell you the mystery of the woman, and of the beast with seven heads and ten horns that carries her. ⁸The beast that you saw was, and is not, and is about to ascend from the bottomless pit and go to destruction. And the inhabitants of the earth, whose names have not been written in the book of life from the foundation of the world, will be amazed when they see the beast, because it was and is not and is to come.

⁹"This calls for a mind that has wisdom: the seven heads are seven mountains on which the woman is seated; also, they are seven kings, ¹⁰of whom five have fallen, one is living, and the other has not yet come; and when he comes, he must remain only a little while. ¹¹As for the beast that was and is not, it is an eighth but it belongs to the seven, and it goes to destruction. ¹²And the ten horns that you saw are ten kings who have not yet received a kingdom, but they are to receive authority as kings for one hour, together with the beast. ¹³These are united in yielding their power and authority to the beast; ¹⁴they will make war on the Lamb, and the Lamb will conquer them, for he is Lord of lords and King of kings, and those with him are called and chosen and faithful."

¹⁵And he said to me, "The waters that you saw, where the whore is seated, are peoples and multitudes and nations and languages. ¹⁶And the ten horns that you saw, they and the beast will hate the whore; they will make her desolate and naked; they will devour her flesh and burn her up with fire. ¹⁷For God has put it into their hearts to carry out his purpose by agreeing to give their kingdom to the beast, until the words of God will be fulfilled. ¹⁸The woman you saw is the great city that rules over the kings of the earth."

John's vision of the great whore sitting on the scarlet beast (verse 3) is a strong contrast to that of the heavenly woman with the crown of twelve stars (12:1). The whore is elaborately described, "clothed in purple and scarlet, and adorned with gold and jewels and pearls" (verse 4). The rulers of the earth have committed fornication with her (verse 2), and she is "drunk with the blood of the saints and the blood of the witnesses to Jesus" (verse 6). The dragon that had sought to devour the newborn child of the heavenly women and make war on the rest of her children is now the vehicle for the whore's gaudy romp. The two women represent faithfulness to God and unfaithfulness, symbolized as prostitution. Clearly one cannot be both a child of the woman with the crown of twelve stars and a customer of the garish woman who sits on the beast.

The prostitute and the beast symbolize the demonic powers of evil that can become entrenched in worldly political and economic systems. On the forehead of the woman is written "Babylon the great, mother of whores and of earth's abominations" (verse 5). In the Old Testament, Babylon was the capital of an empire that destroyed Jerusalem in 587 B.C., thereby becoming a symbol of all the forces hostile to God's people. Throughout history this demonic power has found other incarnations. In John's day it was particularly embodied in the Roman empire. Rome was another Babylon, the source of seductive luxury, deceit, idolatry, and persecution.

After John's vision, the interpreting angel revealed to John "the mystery of the woman and of the beast" (verse 7). The evil woman is revealed as "the great city that rules over the kings of the earth" (verse 18). Furthermore, the seven heads of the beast are revealed as "seven mountains on which the women is seated" (verse 9). Both of these references seem to point to the city of Rome, with its famous seven hills and its supremacy over all the powers of the world. The seven heads of the beast, representing seven kings, may be the succession of Caesars, the contemporary exemplars of the ruling elite opposed to the values of God's kingdom. Yet a literal identification of the woman and the beast with the Roman empire of the first century must not take away from the vision's power as a timeless metaphor of corrupt control that denies the supremacy of God's Lamb.

Despite the amazement produced by the prostitute and the beast in all who look upon them, their power is temporary and their destiny is not salvation but destruction (verse 8). For all its short-term intoxications, the seduction of the earth's inhabitants by the prostitute will lead to devastation. The company she keeps actually hates her and will help destroy her (verse 16). She is left desolate and naked, her flesh eaten and burned with fire by those very kings over whom she ruled. All who belong to the beast are deceptive and self-destructive (verse 17). Evil turns upon itself and performs the purpose that God has announced: the end of evil and the coming of God's reign.

Reflection and discussion

• In what way is the woman riding on the beast both enticing and repulsive? How is evil both attractive and revolting?

• Why is Babylon symbolized by the great harlot? How is Babylon itself also a symbol?

• In what ways can prosperity lure me into placing my trust in material wealth rather than in God?

• In what way does evil turn on itself and become self-destructive? How have I seen this in the Babylons of today's world?

Prayer

Lord of lords and King of kings, you have called and chosen me to be faithful. Give me wisdom to see the world as you see it, to value what you value, to love what you love. Help me to avoid being deceived by things that only seem attractive and desirable.

The light of a lamp will shine in you no more; and the voice of bridegroom and bride will be heard in you no more. Rev 18:23

Fallen Is Babylon the Great

REVELATION 18:1–24 *¹After this I saw another angel coming down from heaven, having great authority; and the earth was made bright with his splendor. ²He called out with a mighty voice,*

"Fallen, fallen is Babylon the great!
   It has become a dwelling place of demons,
a haunt of every foul spirit,
   a haunt of every foul bird,
   a haunt of every foul and hateful beast.
³For all the nations have drunk
   of the wine of the wrath of her fornication,
and the kings of the earth have committed fornication with her,
   and the merchants of the earth have grown rich from the power of her luxury."
⁴Then I heard another voice from heaven saying,
"Come out of her, my people,
   so that you do not take part in her sins,
   and so that you do not share in her plagues;
⁵for her sins are heaped high as heaven,
   and God has remembered her iniquities.
⁶Render to her as she herself has rendered,

and repay her double for her deeds;
   mix a double draught for her in the cup she mixed.
⁷As she glorified herself and lived luxuriously,
   so give her a like measure of torment and grief.
Since in her heart she says,
  'I rule as a queen;
I am no widow,
  and I will never see grief,'
⁸therefore her plagues will come in a single day—
   pestilence and mourning and famine—
and she will be burned with fire;
   for mighty is the Lord God who judges her."

⁹And the kings of the earth, who committed fornication and lived in luxury with her, will weep and wail over her when they see the smoke of her burning; ¹⁰they will stand far off, in fear of her torment, and say,

"Alas, alas, the great city,
   Babylon, the mighty city!
For in one hour your judgment has come."

¹¹And the merchants of the earth weep and mourn for her, since no one buys their cargo anymore, ¹²cargo of gold, silver, jewels and pearls, fine linen, purple, silk and scarlet, all kinds of scented wood, all articles of ivory, all articles of costly wood, bronze, iron, and marble, ¹³cinnamon, spice, incense, myrrh, frankincense, wine, olive oil, choice flour and wheat, cattle and sheep, horses and chariots, slaves—and human lives.

¹⁴"The fruit for which your soul longed
   has gone from you,
and all your dainties and your splendor
   are lost to you,
   never to be found again!"

¹⁵The merchants of these wares, who gained wealth from her, will stand far off, in fear of her torment, weeping and mourning aloud,

¹⁶"Alas, alas, the great city,
   clothed in fine linen,
    in purple and scarlet,
   adorned with gold,
    with jewels, and with pearls!

[17] *For in one hour all this wealth has been laid waste!"*

And all shipmasters and seafarers, sailors and all whose trade is on the sea, stood far off [18] *and cried out as they saw the smoke of her burning,*

"What city was like the great city?"

[19] *And they threw dust on their heads, as they wept and mourned, crying out,*

"Alas, alas, the great city,

where all who had ships at sea

grew rich by her wealth!

For in one hour she has been laid waste."

[20] *Rejoice over her, O heaven, you saints and apostles and prophets! For God has given judgment for you against her.*

[21] *Then a mighty angel took up a stone like a great millstone and threw it into the sea, saying,*

"With such violence Babylon the great city

will be thrown down,

and will be found no more;

[22] *and the sound of harpists and minstrels and of flutists and trumpeters*

will be heard in you no more;

and an artisan of any trade

will be found in you no more;

and the sound of the millstone

will be heard in you no more;

[23] *and the light of a lamp*

will shine in you no more;

and the voice of bridegroom and bride

will be heard in you no more;

for your merchants were the magnates of the earth,

and all nations were deceived by your sorcery.

[24] *And in you was found the blood of prophets and of saints,*

and of all who have been slaughtered on earth."

Another angel comes from heaven to sing a lament over the fall of the great city: "Fallen, fallen is Babylon the great!" (verse 2). The prophet Isaiah used this same refrain to announce the fall of the historical Babylon (Isa 21:9). Through the Lamb, God brings his authority to bear, and the powers of evil are transformed from arrogant opulence to utter desolation. The city is mourned in the same way that the prophets of the Hebrew Scriptures sang of the doom to befall other nations and cities that opposed God. The lament is repeated throughout: "Alas, alas, the great city" (verses 10, 16, 19).

Those who had prospered in her wealth mourned the great city: the kings of the earth (verse 9), the merchants (verse 11), and the shipmasters and seafarers (verse 17). John notes somewhat sarcastically that they weep for her while they "stand far off" (verses 10, 15, 17). They were her lovers while she prospered, but they keep their distance in her death throes. Sin creates no lasting loyalties.

A long list of luxuries traded throughout the empire gives us a glimpse of the vast wealth of the Roman empire. The wealthiest citizens competed to outdo one another in extravagance. At the end of this long list John mentions slaves (verses 12–13). Then, as if to emphasize the reality, he states "and human lives." As many as half the members of society in the Roman empire were slaves. It was only the forced labor of millions of men and women that made possible the comforts of the few.

The heavenly voice urged followers of Jesus to "Come out of her, my people" (verse 4). The cry echoes the call of the ancient exodus. It was not a demand to physically withdraw from the city, but to reject her values, her materialism and exploitation of people. A power built on pride and reckless excess is ultimately hollow and cannot last. In the face of such idolatry, the role of the Lamb's followers was not to topple the empire, but to simply be faithful witnesses.

The fall of the sinful city has a message for any period of history that glorifies material wealth, military power, racial dominance, unbridled consumerism, or any other form of idolatry. John's visions speak to all governments, corporations, institutions, denominations, and bureaucracies that covet power, wealth, and influence. Because we are a part of these systems, we must keep our priorities focused and our vision clear.

Reflection and discussion

• What was wrong with the "Babylon" of this lament? Why was its destruction inevitable?

• Can I see parallels in my own society to the materialism and economic injustice of ancient Rome?

• How often do my own values reflect the materialism and idolatry of Babylon rather than the values of the gospel?

• In whom or what do I place my trust? What can I do to clarify my priorities and act on them?

Prayer

Just God, you are the Lord of all the powers of this world. Help me to recognize and put aside anything that keeps me from you. Help me to form values based on justice and love rather than greed.

SUGGESTIONS FOR FACILITATORS, GROUP SESSION 5

1. Welcome group members and ask if anyone has any questions, announcements, or requests.

2. You may want to pray this prayer as a group:

Lord Jesus Christ, you are the Lord of the harvest, the king of the nations, the Lord of lords and King of kings. We stand before you, sealed on our foreheads with the assurance that we belong to you. We know that the seductive powers of this world are fleeting and doomed for destruction, and we know that your judgment is merciful and true. May we turn to the heavenly woman with the crown of twelve stars as our true mother and turn away from the great harlot who rides on the beast. May we sing together the Lamb's new song of redemption because we know that our victory is assured.

3. Ask one or more of the following questions:
   • What most intrigued you from this week's study?
   • What makes you want to know and understand more of God's word?

4. Discuss lessons 19 through 24. Choose one or more of the questions for reflection and discussion from each lesson to talk over as a group.

5. Ask the group members to name one thing they have most appreciated about the way the group has worked during this Bible study. Ask group members to discuss any changes they might suggest in the way the group works in future studies.

6. Invite group members to complete lessons 25 through 30 on their own during the six days before the next meeting. They should write out their own answers to the questions as preparation for next week's session.

7. Discuss examples of how the words and images of Revelation have influenced art, film, media, and modern culture.

8. Conclude by praying aloud together the prayer at the end of one of the lessons discussed. You may want to conclude the prayer by asking members to voice prayers of thanksgiving.

Hallelujah! For the Lord our God the Almighty reigns. Let us rejoice and exult and give him the glory, for the marriage of the Lamb has come, and his bride has made herself ready; to her it has been granted to be clothed with fine linen, bright and pure. Rev 19:6–8

The Song of Victory

REVELATION 19:1–10 *¹After this I heard what seemed to be the loud voice of a great multitude in heaven, saying,*

"Hallelujah!
Salvation and glory and power to our God,
    ²for his judgments are true and just;
he has judged the great whore
    who corrupted the earth with her fornication,
and he has avenged on her the blood of his servants."
³Once more they said,
"Hallelujah!
The smoke goes up from her forever and ever."
⁴And the twenty-four elders and the four living creatures fell down and worshiped God who is seated on the throne, saying,
"Amen. Hallelujah!"
⁵And from the throne came a voice saying,
"Praise our God,

all you his servants,
and all who fear him,
small and great."

⁶*Then I heard what seemed to be the voice of a great multitude, like the sound of*
many waters and like the sound of mighty thunderpeals, crying out,

"Hallelujah!
For the Lord our God
the Almighty reigns.
⁷*Let us rejoice and exult*
and give him the glory,
for the marriage of the Lamb has come,
and his bride has made herself ready;
⁸*to her it has been granted to be clothed*
with fine linen, bright and pure"—
for the fine linen is the righteous deeds of the saints.

⁹*And the angel said to me, "Write this: Blessed are those who are invited to*
the marriage supper of the Lamb." And he said to me, "These are true words of
God." ¹⁰*Then I fell down at his feet to worship him, but he said to me, "You must*
not do that! I am a fellow servant with you and your comrades who hold the tes-
timony of Jesus. Worship God! For the testimony of Jesus is the spirit of prophecy."

All of Revelation is really about a single reality: because of the slain Lamb, God's reign has triumphed over evil. Now that John's visions have presented evil as finally judged and destroyed, the climactic visions speak only of salvation. The heavenly choruses unite with throngs on earth. They sing of the conquest of evil (verse 2), the coming of God's reign (verse 6), and the wedding feast of the Lamb (verse 7). The vision is a timeless expression of the fullness of God's plan, the complete union of God and his people.

The boundaries separating the worshiping community in heaven and the human one on earth blend together as they shout "Hallelujah" in mutual confirmation that "the Lord our God the Almighty reigns" (verse 6). The joyful liturgy of heaven and earth repeatedly sings "Hallelujah" (verses 1, 3, 4, 6), a Hebrew word meaning "praise the Lord!" The word is found only here in the New Testament, but it is found repeatedly in the book of Psalms, especially the Hallel Psalms (Ps 113–118) sung during the Passover ritual to celebrate the exodus.

The new theme introduced in this triumphant scene is the marriage feast of the Lamb (verses 7–9). Those who have based their lives on God's grace, who have followed the Lamb, will be united with Christ in an embrace of love that will bring life without end. What better symbol of this than a wedding? The nuptial theme is reminiscent of the Old Testament prophets who used the image of marriage to describe the relationship between God and Israel (Hos 2:16–20; Isa 54:5; Ezek 16:8–14). In the gospels Jesus refers to himself as the bridegroom (Matt 9:15) and to the kingdom of God as a wedding feast (Matt 22:1–14). Paul also spoke of marriage as a foreshadowing of the union between Christ and his church (Eph 5:21–33).

John transports us out of the present trials to the end of the age, "for the marriage of the Lamb has come, and his bride has made herself ready" (verse 7). The bride's simple linen apparel, representing "the righteous deeds of the saints" (verse 8), contrasts starkly with the great whore's lavish purple and scarlet robes and jewels. We are invited to envision ourselves as those who have received an invitation to the marriage of God and humanity: "Blessed are those who are invited to the marriage supper of the Lamb" (verse 9). But even more, we are invited to see ourselves as the bride, called to complete and faithful unity with our triumphant Lord.

John intended his book to be read and heard in the eucharistic assembly of the churches. There Christ's past and future coming dissolve in the timeless moment of worship with the angels and saints. In wicked Babylon there will be no more shining lamps, joyful music, or wedding banquets (18:22–23). But the wedding feast of the Lamb and his bride has begun. In its Eucharist the church draws near to the Lamb who was slain, and lives now, and will come again in glory. The church experiences in its worship the joys of eternal union with Christ in the feast of love that lasts forever.

Reflection and discussion

• How does John contrast the prostitute of chapters 17–18 with the bride of the Lamb?

• What aspects of a marriage make it an ideal symbol for the relationship between God and his people?

• What type of marriage preparation should the church use in anticipation of its wedding with Christ?

• In what way is the Christian Eucharist a celebration of the marriage supper of the Lamb?

Prayer

Lamb of God who takes away the sin of the world, how blessed are those called to share in your supper. I rejoice in the embrace of your love and the complete and faithful unity you desire to share with me.

He is clothed in a robe dipped in blood, and his name is called The Word of God. And the armies of heaven, wearing fine linen, white and pure, were following him on white horses. Rev 19:13–14

The King of Kings Riding the White Horse

REVELATION 19:11–21 *¹¹Then I saw heaven opened, and there was a white horse! Its rider is called Faithful and True, and in righteousness he judges and makes war. ¹²His eyes are like a flame of fire, and on his head are many diadems; and he has a name inscribed that no one knows but himself. ¹³He is clothed in a robe dipped in blood, and his name is called The Word of God. ¹⁴And the armies of heaven, wearing fine linen, white and pure, were following him on white horses. ¹⁵From his mouth comes a sharp sword with which to strike down the nations, and he will rule them with a rod of iron; he will tread the wine press of the fury of the wrath of God the Almighty. ¹⁶On his robe and on his thigh he has a name inscribed, "King of kings and Lord of lords."*

¹⁷Then I saw an angel standing in the sun, and with a loud voice he called to all the birds that fly in midheaven, "Come, gather for the great supper of God, ¹⁸to eat the flesh of kings, the flesh of captains, the flesh of the mighty, the flesh of horses and their riders—flesh of all, both free and slave, both small and great." ¹⁹Then I saw the beast and the kings of the earth with their armies gathered to make war against the rider on the horse and against his army. ²⁰And the beast was captured, and with it the false prophet who had performed in its presence the signs by which he deceived those who had received the mark of the beast and those who worshiped its image. These two were thrown alive into the lake of fire that burns with sulfur. [21] *And the rest were killed by the sword of the rider on the horse, the sword that came from his mouth; and all the birds were gorged with their flesh.*

The last time John presented the heavens open, we saw a beautiful woman in distress and a fearsome red dragon (12:1–3). What else should we expect as the heavens open again but a hero riding on a white horse? In this final vision of Christ's victory over the beast, he is depicted as a divine warrior king, with flaming eyes and many crowns (verses 11–12). The images of both the slain Lamb and the conquering warrior express the victory of Christ over the forces of evil.

Yet, this mighty hero does not conquer with violence or vengeance. His robe is not splattered with the blood of his enemies, for the stains are already present as he rides out to meet his foes. His cloak is dipped in his own blood and that of his martyred followers (verse 13) as he charges out to conquer with the power of his self-sacrificing love. His army follows him, dressed in the white linen of faithful discipleship, and armed with only one weapon— the sharp sword that comes from Christ's mouth (verse 15). The messianic forces of Christ and his faithful witnesses destroy the powers of evil with the word of God, the proclamation of the gospel. Throughout all of John's visions, we see that the power that conquers the beast is faithful testimony, patient resistance, generous suffering, and confident trust.

The grotesque feast of flesh eaten by the vultures (verses 17–18) symbolizes the final destruction of earth's idolatry and systems of evil. The forces of evil, the beasts allied with the kings and their armies, are soundly defeated by the victorious Christ (verses 19–21). The beast from the sea and the false prophet (the beast from the land) are captured and cast forever into the lake of fire and sulphur. These two are the first of the "counterfeit trinity" to be thrown into the fiery lake. The satanic dragon will follow (20:10). The rest, those who had received the mark of the beast and worshiped its image, are destroyed by the sword that came from Christ's mouth (verse 21). Since they have rejected the joyful wedding feast of the Lamb, they have become an ugly feast on which the scavengers gorge.

Though the scene is imaginatively gruesome, the meaning is clear. Christ has won the victory and the outcome is certain. The final triumph of Christ means the end of all injustice and human wrongdoing. Those who remain faithful until his coming will share in his victory forever and reap the fruit of his conquest.

Reflection and discussion

• Why is the victory of Christ symbolized by a battle? What convinces me that Christ does not literally fight with violence and bloodshed?

• How is the word of God like a sharp sword? How does God's word help me remain faithful and true?

• Does knowing that Jesus will return to bring God's reign spur me to work for justice in the world? What hopes and frustrations do I feel?

Prayer

Word of God, you pierce my heart with your fervent love. Begin your universal victory here in my own heart. Help me to work for justice and to be faithful and true to your word.

I saw the dead, great and small, standing before the throne, and books were opened. Also another book was opened, the book of life. And the dead were judged according to their works, as recorded in the books. Rev 20:12

Liberation from Evil and Universal Judgment

REVELATION 20:1–15 *¹Then I saw an angel coming down from heaven, holding in his hand the key to the bottomless pit and a great chain. ²He seized the dragon, that ancient serpent, who is the Devil and Satan, and bound him for a thousand years, ³and threw him into the pit, and locked and sealed it over him, so that he would deceive the nations no more, until the thousand years were ended. After that he must be let out for a little while.*

⁴Then I saw thrones, and those seated on them were given authority to judge. I also saw the souls of those who had been beheaded for their testimony to Jesus and for the word of God. They had not worshiped the beast or its image and had not received its mark on their foreheads or their hands. They came to life and reigned with Christ a thousand years. ⁵(The rest of the dead did not come to life until the thousand years were ended.) This is the first resurrection. ⁶Blessed and holy are those who share in the first resurrection. Over these the second death has no power, but they will be priests of God and of Christ, and they will reign with him a thousand years. ⁷When the thousand years are ended, Satan will be released from his prison ⁸and will come out to deceive the nations at the four cor-

ners of the earth, Gog and Magog, in order to gather them for battle; they are as numerous as the sands of the sea. ⁹ They marched up over the breadth of the earth and surrounded the camp of the saints and the beloved city. And fire came down from heaven and consumed them. ¹⁰ And the devil who had deceived them was thrown into the lake of fire and sulfur, where the beast and the false prophet were, and they will be tormented day and night forever and ever.

¹¹ Then I saw a great white throne and the one who sat on it; the earth and the heaven fled from his presence, and no place was found for them. ¹² And I saw the dead, great and small, standing before the throne, and books were opened. Also another book was opened, the book of life. And the dead were judged according to their works, as recorded in the books. ¹³ And the sea gave up the dead that were in it, Death and Hades gave up the dead that were in them, and all were judged according to what they had done. ¹⁴ Then Death and Hades were thrown into the lake of fire. This is the second death, the lake of fire; ¹⁵ and anyone whose name was not found written in the book of life was thrown into the lake of fire.

The final visions of Revelation form a mosaic of related images taken from the biblical and Jewish traditions to express the final destruction of evil and the eternal reign of Christ. There are seven visions in all, each beginning with the words "then I saw" (19:11, 17, 19; 20:1, 4, 11; 21:1). The previous three visions had pictured the destruction of the two beasts by the rider on the white horse. The present three visions express the obliteration of the ultimate source of all evil—"the dragon, that ancient serpent, who is the Devil and Satan" (verse 2). It would be a mistake to understand this series of seven visions as a sequential series of events that can be plotted on a calendar in chronological time. Each scene is, rather, an imaginative and symbolic depiction of the destruction of the world's evil and the complete fulfillment of God's plan for creation.

The opening vision describes an angel coming from heaven with a key and a chain. The satanic dragon, whose time has finally come (12:12), is bound and cast into the abyss without a struggle (verses 1–3). In this vision, evil is overpowered and imprisoned while Christ reigns on the earth; in the next vision, the devil will be finally destroyed in the same lake of fire where the beasts met their final fate (verse 10).

The most evident hope of the early Christians was not so much individual survival beyond the grave, but the reign of Christ on the earth. They looked forward to the time when Christ would return to rule over all creation. John offers us a symbolic description of that reign in which God's anointed king rules over a creation freed from the deceptive influence of evil (verses 4–6). Christ's faithful witnesses, those who had not worshiped the beast or received its mark, ruled with him as kings, judges, and priests. They are a royal priesthood, a worshiping community, living in the presence of God, mediating between God and the world of his creation.

The time of the dragon's imprisonment and the reign of Christ is described as "a thousand years." Though sometimes interpreted as a definite period of time or a timetable for world events, the number is symbolic, like all the other numbers in Revelation. It is a period unable to be measured, since "with the Lord one day is like a thousand years, and a thousand years are like one day" (2 Peter 3:8; Ps 90:4). The thousand years is John's way of expressing the passing away of evil and the ushering in of eternity. Paul spoke about this same final reality as the reign of Christ "until he has put all his enemies under his feet," including the last enemy which is death (1 Cor 15:23–28).

St. Augustine offered a spiritual interpretation for the thousand year reign as the age of the church: the age that began with Christ's resurrection and that will end with his glorious return. In this present age, Christ has already won victory over Satan and the followers of Christ already reign with him since they have experienced a "first resurrection" in the new life of baptism (verses 5–6). We still await the full experience of Christ's reign when he comes to judge the living and the dead.

The release of Satan from the abyss "for a little while" (verses 3, 7) prepares for the final destruction of evil. He resumes his deception of the nations, and uses the figures of "Gog and Magog," known in Jewish literature as the ultimate enemies of God's people to be destroyed in the final battle (verse 8). Evil is magnified to its fullest in these larger-than-life antagonists before being destroyed forever. But as we have come to expect in Revelation, the "last battle" is no battle at all. There is no other victory than that long since won by God in the cross of Christ. Without any struggle, fire comes from heaven and consumes the enemies of God's people, and the devil is cast into the lake of fire and sulphur forever.

With evil finally destroyed, God's victory is now described as the final judgment. All the dead come to life and stand before the "great white throne" of God's judgment (verse 11). "The great and the small"—all come; these are no exceptions and no deferrals. All are judged according to their works (verses 12–13). Though we have all been enrolled in the "book of life" by God's grace—that is, invited to share in eternal life—we are still judged according to how we responded to that noble call in this world. The "first death" is the end of our physical lives; the "second death" (verse 14) is eternal damnation, the "lake of fire" where Satan, the beasts, and now even death itself are cast forever.

Reflection and discussion

• What indicates that the thousand years do not refer to chronological time? What are the indications that the thousand year reign of Christ has already begun?

• What are the similarities between John's judgment scene (verses 11–15) and the last judgment described in Matthew 25:31–46?

Prayer

Lord God, you have conquered Satan, the spirit of evil in the world, and you have destroyed even death forever. Deliver me from evil and help me to trust in the sufficiency of your grace within me. Help me to live today the way I want to live forever.

See, the home of God is among mortals. He will dwell with them as their God; they will be his peoples, and God himself will be with them; he will wipe every tear from their eyes. Rev 21:3–4

All Creation Renewed and Perfected by Its Creator

REVELATION 21:1–8 *¹Then I saw a new heaven and a new earth; for the first heaven and the first earth had passed away, and the sea was no more. ²And I saw the holy city, the new Jerusalem, coming down out of heaven from God, prepared as a bride adorned for her husband. ³And I heard a loud voice from the throne saying,*

"See, the home of God is among mortals.
He will dwell with them;
they will be his peoples,
and God himself will be with them;
⁴he will wipe every tear from their eyes.
Death will be no more;
mourning and crying and pain will be no more,
for the first things have passed away."

⁵And the one who was seated on the throne said, "See, I am making all things new." Also he said, "Write this, for these words are trustworthy and true." ⁶Then he said to me, "It is done! I am the Alpha and the Omega, the beginning and the

end. To the thirsty I will give water as a gift from the spring of the water of life.
⁷Those who conquer will inherit these things, and I will be their God and they
will be my children. ⁸But as for the cowardly, the faithless, the polluted, the mur-
derers, the fornicators, the sorcerers, the idolaters, and all liars, their place will
be in the lake that burns with fire and sulfur, which is the second death."

The closing two chapters provide a marvelous climax for Revelation and thus for the whole Bible. This final vision is a highly symbolic, beautiful description of creation perfected by its creator. The promise had been given long ago by Isaiah: "I am about to create new heavens and a new earth" (Isa 65:17). Human language is incapable of expressing, and human imagination is incapable of perceiving, the perfection of God's reign over creation. Yet, this does not hinder John from using a variety of metaphors to express the wonder of God's final plan for us.

This renewed creation is characterized by the fact that God's dwells with his people; God makes his home with humanity (verse 3) and cares for his people in all their needs: "He will wipe every tear from their eyes. Death will be no more; mourning and crying and pain will be no more" (verse 4). God himself is the final reality who embraces all things. He is "the Alpha and Omega, the beginning and the end" (verse 6). God does not merely bring the end; God is the End—the completion and perfection of all.

For the second time in the book (1:8), God himself speaks: "See, I am making all things new" (verse 5). The present tense indicates that God is already making things new right now. We have already begun to experience God's presence, his comfort, and new life. Indeed, with the coming of Jesus, God has already begun to dwell with the human race (verse 3; John 1:14). God has already begun a new creation in his Son and in all those who are united with him (verse 5; 2 Cor 5:17). We have already experienced God's life-giving water flowing within us (verse 6; John 7:38). We can already experience the tender parental love of God as his son or daughter (verse 7; Rom 8:14). Even if our experience of God's presence is often faint and fragmentary now, we can find consolation in this vision because we know that what we have experienced dimly will embrace us completely.

Reflection and discussion

• What is the most beautiful sight I have ever seen? Why do words fail when I try to describe it to others?

• What will it be like to live without pain, sin, fear, or death, and with the full presence of God? What glimpses has God given me of the joys that await me?

• Which phrase from the reading strikes me most deeply? What does it mean as God's promise to me?

Prayer

God of compassion and love, you are the beginning and the end. You have created me and you can make me new. Let your Spirit move within me to take away painful memories and grief so that you may refresh and renew my life.

I saw no temple in the city, for its temple is the Lord God the Almighty and the Lamb. And the city has no need of sun or moon to shine on it, for the glory of God is its light, and its lamp is the Lamb. Rev 21:22–23

Presenting the Bride of the Lamb

REVELATION 21:9—22:7 *⁹Then one of the seven angels who had the seven bowls full of the seven last plagues came and said to me, "Come, I will show you the bride, the wife of the Lamb." ¹⁰And in the spirit he carried me away to a great, high mountain and showed me the holy city Jerusalem coming down out of heaven from God. ¹¹It has the glory of God and a radiance like a very rare jewel, like jasper, clear as crystal. ¹²It has a great, high wall with twelve gates, and at the gates twelve angels, and on the gates are inscribed the names of the twelve tribes of the Israelites; ¹³on the east three gates, on the north three gates, on the south three gates, and on the west three gates. ¹⁴And the wall of the city has twelve foundations, and on them are the twelve names of the twelve apostles of the Lamb.*

¹⁵The angel who talked to me had a measuring rod of gold to measure the city and its gates and walls. ¹⁶The city lies foursquare, its length the same as its width; and he measured the city with his rod, fifteen hundred miles; its length and width and height are equal. ¹⁷He also measured its wall, one hundred forty-four cubits by human measurement, which the angel was using. ¹⁸The wall is built of jasper, while the city is pure gold, clear as glass. ¹⁹The foundations of the wall of the city are adorned with every jewel; the first was jasper, the second sapphire, the third agate, the fourth emerald, ²⁰the fifth onyx, the sixth carnelian, the seventh chrysolite, the eighth beryl, the ninth topaz, the tenth chrysoprase, the eleventh jacinth, the twelfth amethyst. ²¹And the twelve gates are twelve pearls, each of the gates is a single pearl, and the street of the city is pure gold, transparent as glass.

²²I saw no temple in the city, for its temple is the Lord God the Almighty and the Lamb. ²³And the city has no need of sun or moon to shine on it, for the glory of God is its light, and its lamp is the Lamb. ²⁴The nations will walk by its light, and the kings of the earth will bring their glory into it. ²⁵Its gates will never be shut by day—and there will be no night there. ²⁶People will bring into it the glory and the honor of the nations. ²⁷But nothing unclean will enter it, nor anyone who practices abomination or falsehood, but only those who are written in the Lamb's book of life.

22 ¹Then the angel showed me the river of the water of life, bright as crystal, flowing from the throne of God and of the Lamb ²through the middle of the street of the city. On either side of the river is the tree of life with its twelve kinds of fruit, producing its fruit each month; and the leaves of the tree are for the healing of the nations. ³Nothing accursed will be found there any more. But the throne of God and of the Lamb will be in it, and his servants will worship him; ⁴they will see his face, and his name will be on their foreheads. ⁵And there will be no more night; they need no light of lamp or sun, for the Lord God will be their light, and they will reign forever and ever.

⁶And he said to me, "These words are trustworthy and true, for the Lord, the God of the spirits of the prophets, has sent his angel to show his servants what must soon take place." ⁷"See, I am coming soon! Blessed is the one who keeps the words of the prophecy of this book."

One of the seven angels who had invited John to view the great whore (17:1) also beckons him to see the bride (21:9). The parallelism of the invitations reminds us of the contrast between the harlot and the bride. The texts insist that we face a basic choice in life: we must choose between good and evil, between God's will and the entrapments of the world, between the Lamb and the beasts, between eternal happiness and endless misery.

The bride of the Lamb is also a heavenly city, the new Jerusalem (verse 10). Its description is a tapestry of rich, biblical symbolism. The number twelve is repeated again and again (21:12–14), reminding us of the twelve patriarchs of ancient Israel and the twelve apostles, the people of God fulfilled and perfected. The city is perfectly proportioned—a cube shape, the shape of the holy of holies in Solomon's temple (21:15–16; 1 Kings 6:20). The new Jerusalem, however, has no need of a temple because the city itself is the sanctuary of God's presence (21:22). No longer is God in a reserved place, entered only by the high priest, but God's presence is now accessible to all people and permeates all things. Unlike the gates of earthly cities which are closed at night and in times of danger, the gates of the new city are always open (21:25).

The new Jerusalem symbolizes the complete fulfillment of God's plan for our salvation. It is Paradise restored, with a river flowing through it and the tree of life that grew in Eden blooming in its streets and bearing twelve kinds of fruit (22:1–2; Gen 2:9–10). This city needs no sun or moon or lamps, for God is its light and the Lamb is its lamp (21:23; 22:5).

In the midst of this perfected creation is the throne of God and the Lamb. There we will worship God and see his face; we will be with God, know him completely, and trust in him. God's name will be on our foreheads, signifying that we belong to God and are precious to him (22:3–4). To be a resident of this city is not merely to have a vision of God, as John has been communicating to us, but to be with God, to be in God, in such an intimate way that human language falters when trying to express its wonders.

The vision teaches us that what God has in store for us fulfills all the hopes of Scripture. The prophetic visions of creation's destiny expressed throughout the Bible have reached their fullest development. After all the sound and fury of Revelation's visions, God has the last word, and it is a word of life. Beyond all the tears and pain of humanity's history, men and women find life with God and "they will reign for ever and ever" (22:5). After many images of God's righteous anger and fierce justice, we are left with a final picture of God's unimaginable mercy and love.

Reflection and discussion

• What image of the new Jerusalem impresses me the most? What does this image say to me about God's purpose and plan?

• Why is God's saving plan for us symbolized as both a beautiful bride and a wondrous city?

• Why is there no temple in the new Jerusalem?

• What experiences have especially expressed God's presence and goodness to me? Could I imagine those experiences expanded infinitely as a picture of what God has in store for me eternally?

Prayer

Merciful and loving God, you provide for all your creatures and you give me all that I need. Help me to long for your kingdom and anticipate the good things you have in store for me.

See, I am coming soon; my reward is with me, to repay according to every-one's work. I am the Alpha and the Omega, the first and the last, the beginning and the end. Rev 22:12–13

Come, Lord Jesus

REVELATION 22:8–21 ⁸*I, John, am the one who heard and saw these things. And when I heard and saw them, I fell down to worship at the feet of the angel who showed them to me;* ⁹*but he said to me, "You must not do that! I am a fellow servant with you and your comrades the prophets, and with those who keep the words of this book. Worship God!"*

¹⁰*And he said to me, "Do not seal up the words of the prophecy of this book, for the time is near.* ¹¹*Let the evildoer still do evil, and the filthy still be filthy, and the righteous still do right, and the holy still be holy."*

¹²*"See, I am coming soon; my reward is with me, to repay according to every-one's work.* ¹³*I am the Alpha and the Omega, the first and the last, the beginning and the end."*

¹⁴*Blessed are those who wash their robes, so that they will have the right to the tree of life and may enter the city by the gates.* ¹⁵*Outside are the dogs and sorcerers and fornicators and murderers and idolaters, and everyone who loves and practices falsehood.* ¹⁶*"It is I, Jesus, who sent my angel to you with this testimony for the churches. I am the root and the descendant of David, the bright morning star."*

¹⁷*The Spirit and the bride say, "Come."*

And let everyone who hears say, "Come."

And let everyone who is thirsty come.

Let anyone who wishes take the water of life as a gift.

[18]*I warn everyone who hears the words of the prophecy of this book: if anyone adds to them, God will add to that person the plagues described in this book;* [19]*if anyone takes away from the words of the book of this prophecy, God will take away that person's share in the tree of life and in the holy city, which are described in this book.*

[20]*The one who testifies to these things says, "Surely I am coming soon."*

Amen. Come, Lord Jesus!

[21]*The grace of the Lord Jesus be with all the saints. Amen.*

One last time John presents the contrast between the wonders of salvation (verse 14) and the ugliness of rebellion against God (verse 15). The fundamental choice between the Lamb and the beasts is ours, and we manifest our choice by the deeds of our lives (verse 12). John has tried throughout the book of Revelation to fill us with confidence in Christ's ultimate victory, so that we will choose to follow him wherever he leads us. Jesus is the Lamb who conquered evil through his own weakness, suffering, and death, and who will work through our own weakness, suffering, and death to overturn the deceptions and injustices of the world. Jesus is the beginning and the end of all desire (verse 13); he is the "bright morning star" whose rising begins the never-ending day of eternity (verse 16).

One clear message that comes across in these final verses is the urgency of Revelation. Other apocalyptic writings often include a warning to seal them up for the distant future (Dan 8:26; 12:4). But John is told, "Do not seal up the words of the prophecy of this book, for the time is near" (verse 10). Why the urgency? Three times in the final verses Jesus tells us "I am coming soon!" (verses 7, 12, 20). How should we understand these words of Jesus? They were not addressed to John's first readers as a promise that the world would end soon, for it did not. Nor are they addressed to us today as a prediction about the pending end. We must understand these words of Jesus in a way that both was true for John's readers and is true for us today. The imminence of his coming is not a matter chronological time—indeed nearly two millennia have passed since the book was written. Jesus is not so much speaking about when he is returning as how we are to await his coming. It is the equivalent of the teaching of Jesus in the gospels: "Keep awake therefore, for you do not know on what day your Lord is coming. You must be ready, for the Son of Man is coming at an unexpected hour" (Matt 24:42, 44). We are called by the wisdom of God's inspired word to live as if Jesus were returning today, as if we were to give an account of our lives to God in the next hour. God's kingdom has already drawn near to us, and God wants us to live in anticipation of its full arrival. Through the gift of God's Spirit, God shares with us his own longing for the fulfillment of his plans (verse 17).

When the seven churches to whom John wrote finished reading his letter, they would roll up the scroll and continue with their celebration of the Eucharist on the Lord's day. The final prayer of Revelation—indeed of the Bible—"Come, Lord Jesus!" (verse 20) would sound in their ears. The acclamation is one of the oldest Christian prayers, proclaimed in the liturgy of the early church. In the Lord's Supper we anticipate the supper of the Lamb (19:9). In every Eucharist we celebrate the mystery that Christ, who died and rose for us, will come to us again. We receive the grace (verse 21) that enables us to follow him until he comes in glory.

Reflection and discussion

• How do I understand the meaning of the eucharistic acclamation of the early church, "Come, Lord Jesus"?

• How would my life be different if I knew that Christ was coming in glory tomorrow? What is preventing me from living that way today?

• What does it mean to address Jesus as the Alpha and the Omega?

• These verses call Jesus by several other names: the beginning and the end, the root of David, and the bright morning star. What other titles of Jesus are found in this book?

• What is the most important insight that I have received from studying the book of Revelation?

Prayer

> *Come, Lord Jesus. Come into my heart this day. Fill me with your light and give me the grace to live each day in anticipation of your glorious coming. Amen. Come, Lord Jesus.*

SUGGESTIONS FOR FACILITATORS, GROUP SESSION 6

1. Welcome group members and make any final announcements or requests.

2. You may want to pray this prayer as a group:

Lamb of God, all creation in heaven and on earth rightly gives you praise. You are the beginning and the end, the source and summit of all creation. We long for your final triumph over evil when you will bring your creation to its glorious completion. When you come in glory, gather us into your kingdom where you live with the Father and the Holy Spirit in eternal glory. There we will join with all the angels and saints to adore your majesty and to rejoice in your presence forever. Send your Spirit upon us as we study your word and bless us with inspiration, generosity, and love for one another.

3. Ask one or more of the following questions:
   • How has this study of the book of Revelation helped your life in Christ?
   • In what way has this study challenged you the most?

4. Discuss lessons 25 through 30. Choose one or more of the questions for reflection and discussion from each lesson to discuss as a group.

5. Ask the group if they would like to study another in the Threshold Bible Study series. Discuss the topic and dates, and make a decision among those interested. Ask the group members to suggest people they would like to invite to participate in the next study series.

6. Ask the group to discuss the insights that stand out most from this study over the past six weeks.

7. Conclude by praying aloud the following prayer or another of your own choosing:

Holy Spirit of the living God, you inspired the writers of the Scriptures and you have guided our study during these weeks. Continue to deepen our love for the word of God in the holy Scriptures and draw us more deeply into the heart of Jesus. We thank you for the hope and assurance you have given us through John, your visionary. Through this study, lead us to worship and witness more fully and fervently, and bless us now and always with the fire of your love.

Ordering Additional Studies

Upcoming and Available Threshold Titles
Eucharist
Angels of God
Pilgrimage in the Footsteps of Jesus
Jerusalem, the Holy City
The Names of Jesus
Advent Light
The Tragic and Triumphant Cross
People of the Passion
The Resurrection and the Life
The Mysteries of the Rosary
The Feasts of Judaism
The Sacred Heart of Jesus
The Holy Spirit and Spiritual Gifts
Stewardship of the Earth

To check availability and publication dates, or for a description of each study, visit our website at www.23rdpublications.com or call us at 1-800-321-0411.

Threshold Bible Study is available through your local bookstore or directly from the publisher. The following volume discounts are available from the publisher:

$12.95   (1-3 copies)
$11.95   (4-7 copies)
$10.95   (8-11 copies)
$9.95   (12 or more copies)